T0273887

RURAL IOWA
SAUSAGE

RURAL IOWA
SAUSAGE

HISTORY & TRADITION OF BRATS ON THE BACK ROADS

JAY GOODVIN

AMERICAN PALATE

Published by American Palate
A Division of The History Press
Charleston, SC
www.historypress.com

Copyright © 2023 by Jay Goodvin
All rights reserved

Unless otherwise specified, all images are from the author's collection.

First published 2023

Manufactured in the United States

ISBN 9781467148542

Library of Congress Control Number: 2023940769

Notice: The information in this book is true and complete to the best of our knowledge. It is offered without guarantee on the part of the author or The History Press. The author and The History Press disclaim all liability in connection with the use of this book.

All rights reserved. No part of this book may be reproduced or transmitted in any form whatsoever without prior written permission from the publisher except in the case of brief quotations embodied in critical articles and reviews.

CONTENTS

CONTENTS

ACKNOWLEDGEMENTS

Holy smokes am I honored to present this book to all the folks out there who love their local meat shops, lockers, Main Street USA, Iowa's amazing communities, road trips, history and heritage. You can experience all those elements and more whenever you visit these small family-owned businesses. When you take bundles of custom cuts and sausages home, you can start to reimagine the generations of folks who prepared the precious recipes day after day and the scores of customers who flocked to these meaty destinations for decades. I'll never grow tired of seeking out these wonderful and vital establishments. Keep up all your hard work wherever you are, and I can't wait to reconnect with all of you and keep meeting the men and women behind the counters.

It's funny to think that I would have to narrow this section down because I don't want to. That may sound a little cliché, but it's the truth. Right now, I'm thinking about some of the first places we wandered into in 2018 when I decided to go on the ultimate quest for Iowa's delicious sausages. S&S Meats & Spirts rings a bell. We were traveling all over North Iowa and randomly found ourselves in Osage. Out the corner of my eye, I saw S&S's front signage calling to our carload of Goodvins. The unofficial welcoming committee filed in, and we were off and running with another meaty destination on this continual road trip of a lifetime. I will never forget their hospitality and excitement for what we were doing in the spontaneous moment they met us.

I remember my first visit to Anita Meat Processing when I saw a woman cutting steaks while wearing an Iowa Hawkeye Tiger Hawk logo on her hard hat. I was only there for a few minutes, but that scene has always stuck out within my memory banks.

Then there was the time I met two incredibly energetic ladies at the Amana Smokehouse who couldn't wait to give me a sample of their horseradish jelly on a piece of their legendary smoked ham. A jar of that jelly and several smoked pork chops went home with us to Iowa City on that day.

I haven't always been able to get the names of everyone I've met throughout the years during this tasty road trip, but I genuinely thank all of you and think about the times I've wandered in. I often wonder where you all are and how you're doing these days. It might have been only a few moments but helped me stay on course and keep doing what I absolutely love.

Well, here it goes. It's time I spell out a brief list of people who have inspired me the most through the creation of this book and during the years that led up to it. All of you deserve your own book, and I mean that wholeheartedly.

To my late grandfather Ray Nellis, who has always been one of my greatest mentors, heroes and cherished role models. His skillful knife wielding paired with the endless knowledge of anything food related was an early inspiration for my love of cooking. His boundless intellect with anything I could ask him about was always the greatest gift he ever passed down. I know I would have adored the locker he operated in the town of Early, Iowa, before the grandkids started coming around.

To Adam Polashek of Polashek's Locker Services in Protivin, Iowa. Adam greeted me when I showed up to the locker looking for brats, and it's there where I came up with the idea of traveling the state to find the best sausages. Our "wurst road trip" began there in rural Howard County.

My late father in-law, Reyes Hernandez, with a towering triple-decker cheddar bratwurst BLT with a blue cheese mayo. This picture was taken back in 2018, with all the meat coming from the Gilbertville Locker. One of the tastiest road trips we had ever been on.

To Jeff Hodges of the Minden Meat Market in Minden, Iowa. It was in front of his case of beautiful steaks that the idea of this book was hatched. In the first few minutes of meeting him, I was reminded of how important these businesses are and how few our home state has left.

To the folks at the Midwest Travel Network who encouraged me and many others to keep going with our travels throughout the years and the thoughtfulness the network exuded during the peak of the pandemic when the travel industry was reeling.

To the countless locals who made every step of our journeys possible. Your personalities helped create this book and every road trip we've ever dove into. The rush of memories I get when I think of you can be pleasantly overwhelming because I can imagine so many at one time with every glance at the map.

To my wife, Monica; our son, Charlie; and two daughters, Leah and Gigi, who have been encouraging me to proceed with our adventures. They have joined me for countless miles and have been the beneficiaries of many of the wonderful meals we prepared at home with meats from Iowa meat shops and lockers. I love you all and every memory produced during our gallivants together.

To my late father-in-law, Reyes Hernandez. One of the greatest sports I could have had during a weeklong quest across Eastern Iowa in the chilly early spring of 2018. We hit up several lockers, and he marveled over every meal we made that week with different styles of sausages for breakfast, lunch and supper. I absolutely loved cooking for him, and we'll never forget his gratitude and smile with every plateful he enjoyed.

INTRODUCTION

Think of old pictures of meat being cured in the open air dangling above proud owners and their small assembly of workers standing upright for a few moments for the sake of the photo op. When the flash was complete, it was back to looking down at the cutting board to fashion the popular cuts at the time, carefully creating links through the sausage grinder or calculating each motion with a powerful saw before maneuvering through a side of beef hundreds of pounds heavy. Those pictures from the 1800s to the early days of the twentieth century drip with nostalgia like a pork belly in a smoker, and you begin to make the attempt to relate to the folks looking straight into the lens. Many of the men sport a handlebar mustache and a stark-white apron, knowing full well it was about to be caked with anything after the photographer was finished. They called it Victorian times, and the era brings the assumption of opulence to most people. However, very few lived in that fashion. They raised their families and communities through hard work and perseverance, with the local locker or meat shops supplying the centerpieces of local fare raised by nearby farms. They also connected their customers to a culture they remember in a country they'll never see again. There were few smiles in the pictures of those days, due to the need to remain as still as possible so the memory would take to the shutters of the cameras. The emotions of the business owners and their staff were in the details of the products around them when looked at closely.

For most of the lockers, in that era, the employees were family members learning the trade from the elders, who passed on the skills they learned in Iowa and the old country they once called home. The eyes of people in the photos of the late nineteenth and early twentieth centuries were always later developed in amazing detail; they seemed to look directly at the future generations that would someday see the photo decades later. Consider the knife set neatly arranged that they hoped would last far beyond their time on earth or the steel hooks holding up slaughtered livestock from a loyal customer to keep his farming family and hired hands fed. The same hooks would hang meat getting prepped for CCC workers, then World War II rations for U.S. troops and our allies, eventually bringing the last side of beef or pork to the meat cutters before the business shuttered for good. Some of the old lockers survived many ups and downs but met that lonesome fate. "What if these walls could talk" is an all-too-common phrase for many situations. What if an old coat that hung on a hook near the freezer could tell stories? Imagine the jokes a sturdy wooden butcher block used by generations has heard. And then think of the lonely feelings it might exude from collecting dust in storage because it was now against regulations to be used in the facility. It had been there for so long it nearly grew its own roots into the concrete flooring. Some knives came and went, but the leather strap dangling from the block and the steel hanging from the wall were there from day one and never lost their edge when it came to keeping the edge of all the cutlery. Thousands of laps could have been calculated from fast-moving but carefully orchestrated sharpening techniques. The frequency of a knife being run across a steel could always be heard through any loud machinery, diesel-powered trucks backing up to the locker and the bellowing from customers and workers after a perfectly timed humorous story landed. All objects are without a way to tell their own story, which is why they depend on the people that relied on them to keep their history alive. They were instrumental to keeping so many employed and the family locker running through all degrees of economic times.

In the 1970s, Iowa was up to around 450 lockers statewide. Off-the-beaten-path towns like Baldwin, Holy Cross, Early, Steamboat Rock, Stuart, Donnellson, North English, Sioux Rapids, Aurelia, Randolph, Sutherland, Pleasant Plain, Saint Ansgar and Zwingle are just a handful of communities that cherished a local locker that once welcomed patrons. Children loved the thrill of the huge freezer doors opening to an arctic display of supper items. The larger populations have also missed seeing lockers in cities such as Ottumwa, Iowa City, Council Bluffs, Waterloo, Indianola and more. There are literally hundreds of more Iowa towns that miss the days when they could stop by and see their friends wrapping up their selections and putting in future appointments for the next steer, proud hunting kill or hog that would be ready for slaughter. Iowa is now at just over 100 lockers in operation.

The numbers in their ranks are down, but these amazing and relevant businesses are showing a new generation of consumers just how important these locations are while stressing the necessity of community. The emergence of both small towns and off-the-beaten-path metro neighborhoods can credit many factors to their economic renaissance, with the local locker and butcher being very much a part of it. The average consumer wants to know more about where their meat comes from, how it was raised and how it was processed more than ever. The movement to support local businesses, local producers, local farms and buying local is gaining more steam every day. There is no better way to gather the knowledge you're looking for—when it comes to what you prepare for your family meals—than a stop at one of the lockers and meat shops you come across. And you're expressing your gratitude for Iowa families. The revenue mileage of your purchases at these businesses has more impact than you can imagine. The one-hundred-plus lockers in Iowa are not just surviving. They're innovating, adapting to culinary trends, showcasing classic cuts that are making a comeback, developing unbelievable sausage flavors while maintaining the staples we all love, introducing ethnic delights from modern-day immigrants creating their own Iowa history and keeping the story of Iowa's culture and heritage alive. Their influence is being felt, and they are prepping for a future that brings our lockers back to the forefront.

When you visit a modern-day meaty oasis in places like Yetter, Wayland, Earlville, Corning, Bedford, Parnell, Wever, Harris, West Bend, Frederika, Solon, Cherokee, Dyersville and many more, you can harken back to those old photos of Iowa's early days when the state was still growing up. The facial hair, hat styles, interiors, market pricing, technology, cutting boards and many other things have changed. There's still much that remains the same. The bratwurst your great-grandmother steamed with cabbage may have been processed differently, but the recipe endured. The elaborate stories from regulars aren't exactly the same but similar. The wrist movement of a filet knife from the owner might be operating over a polyethylene-based NSF-certified cutting board, but it's the same technique that was on display when that immovable hardwood butchers block was absorbing its own history from family members years ago.

The exodus of lockers is in the past and should be told in the same breath of how bright the future could be for the ones that remained. It underscores the anticipation of exciting new openings and the future of eager entrepreneurs in the footsteps of the historical ceremony of local meat shops and lockers.

At one point, there were hundreds of local processors all over the state of Iowa. There were over four hundred in the 1970s with the vast majority of our lockers in rural communities all over the map. Fast-forward to the 2020s, and we're now just over one hundred lockers statewide. That means literally hundreds of towns lost a vital local business that was offering a proud service to consumers everywhere. Many of the town lockers were in small communities, employed the locals and brought revenue back into the economy like any restaurant, service station, general store and countless family businesses that have come and gone in Iowa.

Obviously, some of them endured and continue to be important operations to their community into the twenty-first century. Enter the 1970s, with processing regulations updating and affecting local facilities everywhere. Rural Iowa started changing; dwindling populations in small towns and a painful era of farm crisis were on the horizon. The industry this book showcases was hit and hit hard.

Through many years of closures, there are still success stories for many of the lockers and shops. There are some that got their start during a time when folks were shuttering one after the other, with some expanding their operations as the years pile up. Many innovate and appeal to changing demographics, tastes and what the ever-changing consumer palate is gravitating to—all this while some still keep their roots embedded into their craft.

The twenty-first century rolls on with social media helping some of these establishments get the word out into markets where they haven't been able to do so before. Customers are willing to pay shipping costs so they can have the products they remember and love show up to their doorsteps with the flavor of their hometown making it onto their dinner tables and inside their freezers. Neighborhood meat markets are making a comeback as consumers seek locally raised varieties of all kinds, from fresh selections to cured meats and mounds of mouthwatering award-winning jerky with every stop. Old-world flavors with state-of-the-art smokers and original pits still keep up with the demand.

December 2017 showed up and so did a project that I couldn't wait to start. Iowa's Wurst Road Trip: Casing the State for the Best Sausage! I knew it would be a successful exposé of Iowa's sausage makers, but I had no idea how popular it would become. It led us to more of the small towns I love featuring, and I received an education with every stop I made. It was a time when many of the lockers were thriving but still doing their best to stay relevant. Some of them saw a boost in sales from travelers wandering in wanting to shop small and buy local. Some new customers discovered their establishment on social media, even travel shows. A number of local processors were getting their sausages, bologna, luncheon meats and jerky into big-box grocery retailers, helping their bottom line. It was an interesting period of competition, yet with a willingness to stick together, providing support and networking from locker to locker and market to market. It was a time before another event on the horizon would put Iowa's meat suppliers of all sizes front and center locally and internationally.

Spring 2020. COVID-19 hit, and the world was upended. Supply chain issues hit scores of industries across the planet, and markets were unstable at best. By the summer, every community in the United States had seen cases crop up, and the pandemic was running amok within major meatpacking plants. Coronavirus swept through the large workforces that kept these essential plants operating. It was a time of widespread uncertainty of how largescale processing could continue to keep up the pace that was needed with livestock desperately needing to go to market. Major processors begin to temporally shut down to prevent the spread of the virus among their workers and the communities they operate in.

The world still needed to eat, and it was a time when change had to be instituted and quickly. Through the worst health crisis in one hundred years, Iowa's lockers and meat markets saw themselves almost instantly busier than ever, with demand for custom slaughtering skyrocketing. It was a period that illustrated the massive importance that Iowa's local meat shops of all sizes still have and always did. It had an "all hands on deck" feeling, and everyone who handled a knife and steel during the bombardment the pandemic brought has stories about it. Longtime customers made slaughter appointments with a fever pitch that new customers were sharing. Many lockers scheduling two to three years out created a flurry of consumers willing to travel at great length to just get a steer or hog in their freezers.

One of the constants in all the shops throughout my travels is the humor—laughter, jokes, unforgettable anecdotes and the common camaraderie everywhere I went. So many seemed to know each other in this industry, and at times I would relay playful jabs from one locker owner to another. Sometimes lockers were hours away from each other. I feel like I am right in my element at these places and imagine my grandfather's locker in Early, Iowa, being operated in a similar atmosphere. Regular customers can easily "upsell" me when they talk about their own favorite selections and how I can't go home without them. It's the flavors of their hometown. It's the flavors of Iowa.

There is going to be a lot of obvious talk about the destinations on these back roads when it comes to butchering, slaughter, meat cutting and masterful sausage making. Naturally, we think of our favorite lockers, shops and grocery stores for all of our particular selections. If you seek the delicious sausages, then I urge you to look to our local restaurants as well, because many of them are supporting these small businesses by using their products on menus all over that state. Some of Iowa's chefs are creating their own sausage within the kitchens of their popular restaurants as well. Keep an eye out for these talented cooks who love to support the same places we all admire.

We've seen endless miles of Iowa using the popular flavors of brats and other sausages as the driving force at times. One of these miles got us stuck in the mud on the Cass and Audubon County line on a Mother's Day afternoon. After visiting the area, we found ourselves desperate for help, and in fine rural Iowa fashion, a local farmer came to our rescue just minutes after we got stuck. His name was Mike McDermott, and he saved our bacon on that day by towing us out of the mud with his powerful ATV. We followed him back to his farm, where he helped me clean the gunk and rocks off our tires. After a few minutes of spraying down my car, he asked, "Aren't you the bratwurst guy?" I smiled and said, "I sure am," knowing exactly what he was referencing. He'd read up on our adventures and recognized me from our posts and promos. I told him the bratwurst guy needs to use his melon a lot better when he's exploring the country roads. It was a perfect moment for us after a long and entertaining trip in Cass and Audubon Counties. Rural hospitality and the funny side of road tripping filled the day with some of the best memories I have of Western Iowa. Ironically, I bumped into Mike in the town of Anita a month later, where we shared more laughter at the local gas station. This was just one of several reminders I've had that somehow connected our travels to Iowa's lockers and meat shops. To this day, "Bratwurst Guy" is one of my all-time favorite nicknames anyone has ever given me.

I wish we could have fit every locker and meat shop in Iowa into this book, and even more importantly, I wish I could have gotten to all of them and brought home their brats and sausages. I mean there's got to be a ring bologna I haven't had yet. It's time to take a tour around Europe with Iowa's meat-filled destinations as our motor with no passport needed. You've never visited the old country? You're about to!

1

STOPPING FOR LOCKER PIE

DAYTON MEAT PRODUCTS

102 MONTEZUMA STREET, MALCOM, IOWA

(POWESHIEK COUNTY)

There's always going to be adventures when we look for the small towns clear off in the distance where the Wi-Fi may struggle and the nearest metro area is over an hour away. However, our "on-the-beaten-path" travels have yielded incredible visits in small-town Iowa from a just a mile or less from the interstate exits. This would be where we start in this historical tour, and it's in a county that sees thousands of travelers every day.

Malcom is a stone's throw from Newton and Des Moines, which means Dayton Meat Products is bringing a constant stream of customers from its rural Poweshiek County surroundings, a steady flow from some of Central Iowa's metro communities and motorists discovering a facility full of amazing products created by this amazing family business.

There are the classic go-to ways when it comes to a homemade pie craving. Marvelous diners and greasy spoons seem to have some of the greatest of all time, and you find yourself always saving room for a slice. Grandma's house during the holidays can be some of the most nostalgic of memories for oodles of pie. How about when you're picking up your meat bundle at the local locker and you realize there's an opportunity to be the dessert hero when you get home? Going to the locker for pie is a rare errand in most communities, but it's not for the Central Iowa folks who

Two of my favorite items at Dayton Meat Products: their legendary sweet bologna and made-from-scratch pie. Two delicious items that you don't get a chance to see at every locker or meat shop. What's the key ingredient for old school pie recipes? Lard!

know Dayton Meat Products in the Poweshiek County town of Malcom. The aroma of farmland, exhaust from hundreds of cars passing by at seventy-five miles per hour or faster and the Dayton's smoker will fill your senses the moment you open your car door. You'll hear said traffic when you arrive and then the sounds of meat locker USA once you walk through the front door. Chopping, pounding, slicing, a register opening, customers interacting with the employees and always a boisterous pitch in the air. I'm home again. And I've never once resided in Malcom.

Dayton's is directly off of Interstate 80, with an endless stream of motorists that travel past it every day and night. The people who know about Dayton's

Above: What a crew at Dayton's! This Malcom, Iowa establishment is family-oriented and has been since the beginning.

Left: Bill Dayton standing in front of a brand-new, state-of-the-art smoker shipped to Malcom from Germany.

stop in to fill up on road trip snacks like jerky and meat sticks. Many will supply up with the shop's great selection of smoked sausages, brats, bacon and tasty specialties like sweet bologna and breakfast links.

In 1959, there were seven lockers in Poweshiek County alone, including what was called the Malcom Locker, when Lawrence Dayton bought and started operating what is now Dayton Meat Products. It was a family operation from the beginning, as Bill Dayton described: "Five kids grew up in the locker and all worked here." It's a comforting feeling when you listen to Bill talk about the family structure that Dayton's is built on.

The family foundation that started in 1959 is on full display at the present time. Now in a location that was constructed in 1994, the shop's tradition continues into the 2020s. Now, equipped with a state-of-the-art smoker shipped in from Germany, Dayton's is improving its productivity and producing award-winning products year after year. Its keeping intact the flavors that folks have come to recognize for several generations. And then there's the pie…

The art of the mincemeat pie is swirling in the winds of time. Once a staple in just about every state across the country that had a German influence, it is now unknown or even scoffed at in some places. However, there are still fans of this unique pie, and many of them reside near Malcom. What's the key ingredient to the crust? Lard!

Dayton's mincemeat pie is a German recipe that was over one hundred years old when it was handed over to Lawrence Dayton in 1959 when he took over the Malcom Locker. It is still enjoyed today by an untold number of customers. The mincemeat is surrounded by an authentic homemade crust prepared right here at Dayton's, and it is always a top seller.

There's never a bad time to stop into Dayton's, but Fridays are my personal favorite. The workers at this Malcom haven for meaty goodness created an unofficial weekly holiday that I and so many can get the hang of. Every Friday, they wear overalls to bring awareness to everyone who wears overalls, and that's all I personally need to hear to keep going back to Dayton's because I like seeing skilled meat cutters and sausage makers with style.

The sounds from the main entrance are a constant every time I stop into Dayton's. The staff stays busy with customers coming and going, with most of them chatting it up with someone from the Dayton crew. It's a holistic experience mixed with a rush of orders getting processed and bundled. The buzzing of the saw, knives getting sharpened and meat being tenderized naturally make me want to raise the volume of my voice when I'm there as it does for others who want to tell a story or simply talk shop about what's in the coolers and freezers. I like knowing that people can discover little towns like Malcom every day from the never-ending traffic on the interstate if they should choose. Even if they live hours away or even out of state, if they become a random customer at Dayton's, they may be inspired to support their own local locker wherever that might be. That is the goal for so many of these locker owners and operators in this meaty industry all over the map in every state. The more one thrives the more they all get noticed and taken seriously by a hungry nation like ours. American consumers need more families like the Daytons who can handle the stress, constant changes and long hours of the locker business. I mean someone has gotta win some cured meat awards around here.

What we made at home:

Au gratin potatoes with thick-cut Cajun bacon pieces
Slices of sweet bologna on whole wheat crackers and raw horseradish
Fajitas with skinless cheese-filled Polish sausage
Smoky Maple Links with pancakes
Dayton's mixed berry pie

NEARBY AREAS OF INTEREST

The City of Grinnell is home to its proud liberal arts campus, Grinnell College, with an incredible museum. It has plenty of restaurants and shopping and serves as the main entertainment hub for Poweshiek County.

The City of Newton brings in thousands of NASCAR fans, and we know they love to fill up their grills with juicy and meaty delights during their tailgate parties. A longtime local summertime staple is the historic Valle Drive-In movie theater. Go to Newton for the weekend and take in the double feature in a classic Midwest atmosphere.

Historic US Route 6: This national highway has many miles throughout Iowa on its coast-to-coast path. You'll need a snack when you're on this historic route, so get into Malcom and hit up Dayton's before or after visiting the Community of Flags of Brooklyn, Iowa.

IOWA VALLEY SCENIC BYWAY: This beautiful byway winds through the hilly pastures of Central and Eastern Iowa and into many small-town treasures like the Amana Colonies and Marengo.

LINCOLN HIGHWAY HERITAGE BYWAY: Another one of our national treasures when it comes to a coast-to-coast road trip. Close by Malcom are Old 30 cities like Belle Plaine, Tama and Toledo.

OTHER MEAT SHOPS AND LOCKERS IN THE AREA

SULLY LOCKER in Sully, Iowa
COMMUNITY LOCKERS in Victor, Iowa

2

CZECH THIS OUT

POLASHEK'S LOCKER SERVICES

218 SOUTH MAIN STREET, PROTIVIN, IOWA

(HOWARD COUNTY)

One night while channel surfing, I came across *Bizarre Foods America* with Andrew Zimmern. It's a show that I'd watched several times before and casually stopped my clicking when I saw Chef Zimmern's bald melon talking about headcheese. About two minutes went by, and then it dawned on me that he was in Iowa. And not just in Iowa, but a town I never heard of: the little Czech heritage community known as Protivin just south of Cresco in Northeast Iowa. The establishment was Polashek's Locker Services, and the locker instantly made it onto my bucket list of travels.

In the summer of 2017, I found myself shaking hands with the Polashek's crew in person. It was a busy Saturday afternoon in Protivin, and it was where I'd come up with our idea for Iowa's Wurst Road Trip on *The Iowa Gallivant* while talking with Adam Polashek in front of a freezer full of sausages. Among these sausages was a local, Czech delight known as *jaternice*: pork trim, pork snout, pork tongue, barley, cracker crumbs, onions and seasoning all mixed and ground together for a just one of several specialties at Polashek's.

When Paul and Judy became the proud owners of Polashek's Locker Service in 1983, they kept up the long tradition of operating a locker in this rural Northeast Iowa community. To this day, they still use the

Opposite, top: You had me at headcheese, Polashek's! The shop's beef jerky is winning awards, but it was the famous headcheese that piqued the interest of celebrity chef and Travel Channel star Andrew Zimmern and brought him to Protivin, Iowa.

Opposite, bottom: Cory Polashek displaying the calendar of appointments for future slaughter dates, filled up with years of dates booked in advance. This became normal operating procedure for lockers all over Iowa in 2020.

Above: Father Paul (*right*) and son Adam (*left*) semi-surrounded by plaques awarded to Polashek's throughout its forty-year history.

jaternice recipe from Mary Hudecek and offer it in patties, ring and bulk. They still sell countless pounds of their headcheese—which brought in Andrew Zimmern—their popular luncheon meat and more. My personal favorite is the incredible array of brats stuffed with everything from mac and cheese, triple cheese, pineapple, mushrooms and Swiss, bacon and cheddar and more!

Hanging out with Adam, Cory and their father, Paul, while they carefully cut into entire sides of meat is a wonderful way to spend an afternoon with down-to-earth folks I find myself missing at times. By their side is a group of Polashek's employees who all know how to keep the stories, BSing and limitless laughter going. Customers file in to pick up orders, shop around or just visit with the Polashek's crew and for good reason. It has a coffeeshop meetup feel but with a lot more testosterone and way better stories than your run-of-the-mill coffee club. You hear about days when a steer got loose from the kill floor and ran through the entire facility and out the front door just as a customer opened it, unaware of what was going on inside. Luckily, the loyal patron didn't go for a ride himself or worse. This story was told to me over loud bouts of laughter while no one skipped a beat when it came to cutting steaks from a large side of beef hanging beside us. Paul was cooking jaternice nearby for a snack we were all about to enjoy. A scene and story I can always appreciate when I visit Polashek's.

The family aspect continues here at Polashek's Locker and won't really ease up during the course of this book. It's one of the driving forces that put this project together, with the banter passed down just as much as the meat cutting skills and techniques. Polashek's continues to be one of the most welcoming lockers anyone can visit, with the whole family gathered around the cutting boards and huge sides of beef, deer and other livestock. The North Iowa accents come out as they tell the tales of Protivin with

Beef, beef...and more beef! The cutting and trimming never ends with the experts at Polashek's.

the occasional Czech pronunciation of something thrown in. Sure, you can pick the topic of meat when you're there and the Polasheks with their trusty crew will happily tell you everything you want to know. I prefer to talk about anything that's not directly in the locker, however. Getting the Polasheks to start kidding around and bringing up stories completely off topic will always produce a whirlwind of laughter while you're there. They're professional, but they don't shy away from having a good time. The pride they have for Protivin is 100 percent genuine and noticeable when you start getting to know these folks. A heads-up about the annual Czech Days every August in Protivin is almost a guarantee. They want to see their out-of-town customers return to the locker, but our return to Protivin is the main goal for this family. That's a lesson on being an ambassador for any community member and business owner.

What we made at home:

Cheesy jalapeño summer sausage on Ritz crackers
Jaternice hash with scrambled eggs, bacon, toast and sliced tomatoes
Omelet links breakfast tacos
Pan-fried pork belly–bacon patty biscuit breakfast sandwiches with over easy
    eggs, cheese and fried potatoes
Broccoli casserole with cheese-filled brats
Maple breakfast sausage and pancakes
Jaternice shepherd's pie
Headcheese sandwiches on white bread with Miracle Whip

NEARBY POINTS OF INTEREST

The City of Cresco and its important international history. The Norman Borlaug Birthplace Farm is a fascinating glimpse into the childhood home of the man who helped develop "miracle wheat" and was responsible for feeding billions of people worldwide. Cresco is also the birthplace of the world's first flight attendant, the marketing genius who came up with the name for Cheerios, five U.S. Navy admirals and wrestling champions of all levels. It's pretty safe to say that Cresco has produced its fair share of local legends and international celebrities.

The CITY OF DECORAH is a beautiful destination all year long. Positioned among the bluffs of the Driftless Area along the winding Volga River, Decorah has become one of Iowa's most scenic cities. Home to LUTHER COLLEGE, popular breweries and some of Northeast Iowa's most well-known restaurants like MABE'S PIZZA!

OTHER LOCKERS AND MEAT SHOPS IN THE AREA

COUNTY LINE LOCKER in Riceville, Iowa
ELMA LOCKER AND GROCERY in Elma, Iowa
ALTA VISTA MEAT CO in Alta Vista, Iowa
IONIA LOCKER in Ionia, Iowa
FREDERIKA LOCKER in Frederika, Iowa

3

OVER 140 YEARS OF

SMOKY NEW ALBIN

CITY MEAT MARKET

199 RAILROAD AVENUE, NEW ALBIN, IOWA

(ALLAMAKEE COUNTY)

Picture a couple rows of grocery items, beer and pop coolers, camping supplies and a well-oiled crew rattling off descriptions of everything meaty in the cold case. The familiar generosity of samples to new and old customers, butcher paper getting ripped off the roll every few seconds and whiffs of smoked goodies ready to be wrapped. Al's laughter, a customer clowning him and the workers giving it back. The chatter is nonstop and so is the enjoyment of being in one of the furthest reaches of Iowa's territory. The proud son of the operation is a young man named Josh who seems to teleport through the century-old building. One moment he's at the smoker, then all of a sudden at the register; next he's bringing a bundle from the back and grinning at everyone passing by the storefront decorated with colorful autumn mums. I and countless others on this day, and every day, feel right at home in New Albin and the time capsule that is City Meat Market.

The same story has been told by Allamakee County locals for over 140 years: "I come home to visit, and City Meat Market still smells the same." That, my friends, is a compliment and testament to a family business that has been loading its smokers in the most northeastern town in Iowa for generations.

Al (*left*) and Josh (*right*) of City Meat Market in front of their trusty smoker in New Albin, Iowa.

The 1880s saw the massive expansion of the railroad industry, and Iowa was a powerhouse when it came to moving the country's goods all over the map. This is one of the leading reasons why Iowa is absolutely loaded with communities, and New Albin is one of the state's old railroad towns near the Mississippi River. These days, the little town of New Albin sees more tourists and travelers experiencing the Great River Road rather than conductors, crews and passengers stopping before moving on to Minneapolis, Chicago or Dubuque. The economic boom that hit Iowa's river towns and interior brought a host of families that still yearned for the flavors of the old country, and New Albin was no different. One of the area families took over the local meat market in 1882, and it's been in the family ever since.

"I think of Grandpa and Grandma a lot. They laid the groundwork for what we operate today. They'd be amazed to see how much we go through today," said Josh Dreps, one of the operators of City Meat Market, of what he reflects on when it comes to the market he's seen grown in popularity over the years. "They would make fifty to sixty pounds of ring bologna for the week, and that was considered a lot. They even had a sausage maker

Al taking a moment to pose with a rack of freshly smoked ring bologna. One of City Meat Market's most popular creations, it has been making customers smile for generations. It's also been known to make folks homesick for New Albin—good thing City Meat Market ships.

from Germany that worked here awhile and was amazed by the volume that the store could do. Now we do around six hundred pounds a week and still run out. Three thousand pounds during the Christmas season." Josh spent six years in the U.S. Navy and eventually made his own mark in the amazing history of City Meat Market. Josh was leaning into his chair as we sat at the table in the back watching the endless stream of customers lining up to make their selections—a typical sight on a weekend. The back room is a prep area, but it also has the welcoming feel of an old rural kitchen in a farmhouse that could provide its own historical book of stories and tales of New Albin. This is a compelling attribute, but the City Meat Market is nor the only business of its kind to make one feel this way. Josh would soon be making trips downstairs to check on the giant smoker within the foundation of the building. It's not just a meat market and small grocery store. It's also a home.

"Dad likes to say he kicked his parents out of the house when he was fourteen." Josh's usual smile was showing when he mentioned his dad's humor. Al Wuennecke was raised upstairs and continued to occupy the family abode when his parents purchased the house next door to the market. Al raised his own family there, and it's where Josh and his new bride live today. Are Al and Josh close? You bet they are! Both sported mullets that they grew out with the rest of the groomsmen for Josh's recent wedding. Al and Josh's hard work and knowhow underscore a classic sense of humor that regulars and new customers have come to enjoy year after a year. The culture at City Meat Market can most likely be traced as far back as some of its recipes.

This family has been producing many selections throughout its long history, with some of them being offered from day one to modern-day meat lovers. The ring bologna is one of them, and you can't go wrong when getting a package of this Iowa signature wrapped up. Great for a stocking stuffer—seriously! Josh is proud to say that a customer from Chicago gives out City Meat's bacon and bologna every year for Christmas.

The area had plenty of residents with German heritage when New Albin was founded, and you can get a literally taste of New Albin's past with a healthy dose of what they call Gable Links. A doctor loved this style of sausage, and it found a forever home in New Albin; it's been a 140-year staple at City Meat Market with a recipe brought from Germany.

A popular item that locals have come to expect from City Meat Market is what they call Red Dog: the ground eye of round beef with a little onion salt and black pepper. How do you cook it? Scoop a bite and place it on a cracker, and that's all the preparation you need for this dish. It's served raw and always has been. Just ask the local fire department how great the Red Dog is—they have been ordering pounds and pounds of it for annual events.

Kopfwurst is another of City Meat Market's ancient masterpieces, and it's great for both the sweet and savory side of your appetite. The sausage contains cooked beef brisket and sirloin that's ground together with steel-cut oats and allspice. For generations, Al's family has been slicing and sizzling up kopfwurst, then topping it with a little maple syrup. Josh described the syrupy technique as something you start liking the older you get. Hey, if Al says it's gourmet eatin' then I'm going with it! Pass the Red Dog and let's get the day started right in New Albin.

One of the best parts of meeting many of the folks in these places is getting a chance to spend time with them after their workday is done. In New Albin, that means a few beers at the local watering holes. Pulling up a barstool with these guys was a pleasure the last time I was in town, and all the humor at City Meat Market followed. We shared laughs with staff and all the locals we hung out with.

The history of Allamakee County can't be told without the story of City Meat Market and the family that's been running it for generations. They're all still making history and serving as community leaders at the same time in this picturesque corner of Iowa. To get a whiff of the City Meat Market smoker is to get a whiff of New Albin's story and the larger history of Northeast Iowa. Gazing at the architecture of City Market's proud building is what thousands of customers have done every year since the shop was constructed. Al is ready to tell you about every brick, streak of paint, window, nook and cranny of this meat shop. Just stop in and get in line for taste of tradition when it's your turn. Seriously, grab some smoked hard-boiled eggs if they haven't run out. Total life changer.

What we made at home:

Kopfwurst sandwiches on toast with lettuce, tomato and mayonnaise
BLTs with their amazing bacon
Bacon and smoked boiled egg hoagie sandwich topped with local cheese curds

NEARBY POINTS OF INTEREST

DRIFTLESS AREA SCENIC BYWAY: A stunningly beautiful byway that will lead you all over Allamakee County and Winneshiek County to the west. One of the most popular and scenic times of year for this area is during the autumn weeks when the leaves are turning into marvelous colors in its abundant woodlands, parks and forests.

IRON POST HISTORICAL MARKER: You can actually walk to this roadside attraction from City Meat Market. It marks the border with our Minnesota neighbors and is the most northeastern spot you can possibly step foot on in the state of Iowa.

ARMY ROAD: One of the best ways to behold the Upper Mississippi River and its scenic sloughs. Army Road will take you on a ride into the riverside without actually getting wet. You'll be surrounded by the Mississippi River with its vegetation, wildlife, riverbanks and tons of opportunities to take unbelievable pictures.

The CITY OF LANSING, Iowa is "Where Main Street Meets the Mississippi." Bald eagle enthusiasts flock to this town every winter, as do Driftless Area travelers during every season. It is a classic river town with a charming and historic Main Street with treasures you can only find in Lansing like HORSFALL LANSING VARIETY STORE and the SAFE HOUSE SALOON.

MOUNT HOSMER: A bluff in Lansing that gives you a powerful view of the Upper Mississippi River. The islands within the sloughs are in full view, as are the Wisconsin neighbors across the river. I haven't been to every scenic overlook along the thousands of miles of the Mississippi River from Minnesota's Lake Itasca to Louisiana's Gulf Coast. But I can't imagine a greater one than Mount Hosmer in Lansing, Iowa.

OTHER LOCKERS AND MEAT SHOPS IN THE AREA

JET'S MEAT PROCESSING in Waukon, Iowa

4

HAUNTED ROEHRKASSE MEAT CO.

213 WEST WELSH STREET, WILLIAMSBURG, IOWA

(IOWA COUNTY)

It's not often that you walk into a locker or meat market and you hear about things going bump in the night. Or bump in the morning and afternoons. The Jacoby family was eager to talk about Roehrkasse Meat Co. and the long history it's had in the Williamsburg community since 1937.

Colby and his wife, Nancy, have seen objects move and figures lurking around the old meat shop and have come to accept the phenomena. They and their daughter Kayte believe that there's nothing malicious about the spirits, even though the ghosts give off a spooky vibe being in a building full of dangerous objects. Wandering spirits or not, the Jacobys' business is turning out some memorable products every day, and you know I wasn't leaving without a fantastic assortment of their meat products.

The salesroom has a "welcome" home vibe to it with old pictures of the Roehrkasse and Williamsburg past on the walls. Antiques and old knives are also on display, and it gives you a sense of how much the Jacoby family values the history of their proud business. I was a new customer meeting this family for the first time and was shown around the whole shop like they would welcome a guest into their house.

The excitement they have for the importance of this industry doesn't go unnoticed when they begin to talk about how much they love their valued

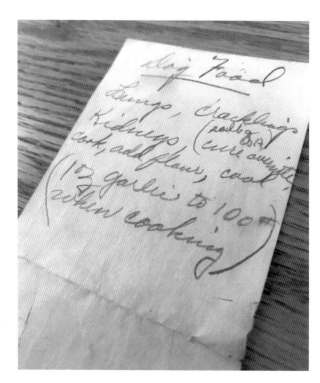

Left: Handwritten dog food recipe consisting of organ meat. This wasn't your average dried kibble that Roehrkasse Meat Co. was making from scratch in the mid-twentieth century.

Below: An old journal filled with original recipes at Roehrkasse's. Summer sausage, dry cure and brine are just a few noted and written down from the 1930s.

Antique knife set still looking sharp. Walking into Roehrkasse's is like stepping into an unofficial Williamsburg, Iowa museum.

Taking a moment to pose for an important picture. They look serious, but I bet they had some of the humor I've gotten used to in Iowa's lockers and meat shops. *Courtesy of Roehrkasse Meat Co.*

customers and the surrounding community. Along with custom processing, Roehrkasse Meat Co. offers many specialties to choose from: brat flavors aplenty like mushroom and Swiss, apple, mango habanero, buffalo blue cheese and more! If you like both traditional and trending flavors, then Roehrkasse's needs to be on your list.

Never mind that voice you heard or that shadow around the corner. Don't be afraid of the sensor-activated hand towel machine spitting out its towels with no one around it. It's just a typical day at Roehrkasse Meat Co. The spooky tales are made better with all the relics of old-fashioned meat cutting hanging on the wall with black and white pictures. Perhaps the eyes on the photographed subjects feel like they're watching and following you throughout the shop. Opening one of the old recipe books or ledgers feels like the beginning of the Roehrkasse story, with its current owners doing a wonderful job illustrating the history day after day on the Williamsburg square. I think I found my go-to Halloween stop this year—locker style.

Keeping the history alive is one of my favorite specialties, and Roehrkasse's does it so well. *Courtesy of Roerkasse Meat Co.*

The Jacobys thanked us for the work we were doing when it comes to featuring the industry they're so proud to be a part of. The exuberant spirit that Nancy gives off is one that makes it irresistible to enjoy. When the owners' excitement pours out, it really does affect the quality of the products. Get over to the Williamsburg town square and see all the spirits of Roehrkasse Meat Co.

What we made at home:

Breakfast sandwich on an everything bagel with sausage-filled hash browns and cheese
Summer sausage on crackers with assorted chili peppers
Smoked pork sausage bites dipped in queso
Twice-baked potatoes with sliced frankfurters

NEARBY POINTS OF INTEREST

WILLIAMSBURG, another historic U.S. Route 6 town, is just a few miles from Interstate 80, which won't give you too much of a detour if you have a set heading. This is one of Iowa's meatiest paths!

Past the large outlet mall is the FIRESIDE WINERY, north of Williamsburg, where you can enjoy award-winning local wines in the beautiful tasting room. Check out this rural retreat for some of Iowa's finest varietals to go with those delicious purchases you just made on the Williamsburg square.

OTHER LOCKERS AND MEAT SHOPS IN THE AREA:

COOK'S MEAT LOCKER in Parnell, Iowa
AMANA MEAT SHOP AND SMOKEHOUSE in Amana, Iowa

5

THE WHOLE ENCHILADA

GRESS LOCKER

202 WEST KIMBALL STREET, HANCOCK, IOWA

(POTTAWATTAMIE COUNTY)

When people think of gourmet Mexican food, we naturally think of our favorite restaurants and authentic taquerias. However, there's a swath of trusty customers in Western Iowa that have their own go-to for the classic enchilada craving, and they're being prepared by the tens of thousands in Hancock, Iowa.

Showing up to this locker for the first time provided an interesting sight. Hancock's bridge was under construction at the time, but that was all right for road trip material. The long way into town is always the way I want to travel, and there was boundless summertime countryside with emerald rows of crops surrounding the hilly blacktop. Upon arrival, I waited my turn to enter Gress Locker with other locals and watched as everyone who walked back to their vehicles held packages of enchiladas, among other selections. I smiled, and one of the customers shouted, "I told you! You gotta take some home, too!" It was my turn to enter and sit across a small desk by the front door and visit.

Gress Locker might be in a small town, but it has a large fanbase that's been growing since 1961 when Cletus Gress opened the doors to the family business. The current location has been serving its customers since 1964 and

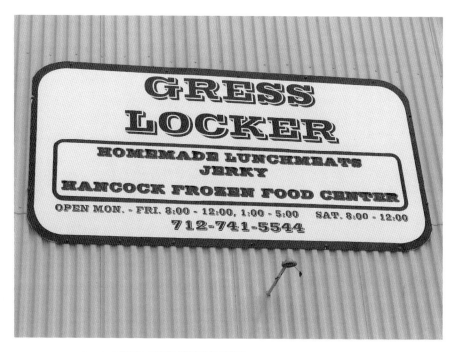

Above: The bright-colored siding pops at the Gress Locker in Hancock, Iowa. So do the flavors in its products.

Left: Gress's 100,000th enchilada was packed on July 7, 2004. *Courtesy of Gress Locker*.

creating a delicious amount of local history into the twenty-first century. Mark Gress is the leader of this establishment and keeps up with some of the German heritage that goes into the creations his father brought to Pottawattamie County in the '60s. Brats of all flavors fill up the orders, as do ring bologna, jerky and spicy selections like ghost pepper sticks. The biggest seller is the popular Iowa tradition of dried beef that's been added to slowly cooked creamy gravy or piled on delicious sandwiches in kitchens for generations.

Mark's dad was the constant mentor for him and everyone who worked side by side with Cletus throughout the years in Hancock. The little town with a spirited locker would go on to create an enchilada niche that's been the add-on to meat bundles for years with no signs of slowing down. "I'd like to schedule a steer for slaughter and while I'm here, I'll take ghost pepper meat sticks and three dozen enchiladas…" That's Hancock, Iowa, right there!

It may not seem like this to others, but getting enchiladas by the dozen is taking a walk on the wild side when it comes to locker exploring. To see the smiles on their faces when you commit to a bundle of these tasty treasures is something to admire as well. Those smiles are telling you that the Gress Loker just got you hooked and they know it. I'm sure enchiladas weren't in the original business model, but everyone is glad they evolved to fill a local niche. That's what Iowa's lockers and meat shops continue to do every year. Whether it's updating equipment, purchasing state-of-the-art smokers, improving recipes, hiring more employees, expanding, building on to existing structures or coming up with modern culinary delights, filling the needs for customers is what these places do best—with each and every one of them evolving through the test of time. One enchilada at a time. Or should I say a dozen at a time?

What we made at home:

Traditional enchiladas topped with melted cheese
Dried beef gravy on toasted English muffins with peas

NEARBY POINTS OF INTEREST

Walnut, Iowa is known as Iowa's Antique City! If you love antiquing, then Walnut needs to be on your shortlist of cities that specialize in this industry. This town has become the premier destination for a nation of collectors, exuding small-town charm and offering something for every type of treasure hunter. Rumor has it that Bob Seger came up with the line "On a long lonesome highway east of Omaha…" at a bar in Walnut, Iowa, long ago. That hasn't been proven, but it's worth investigating.

Griswold, Iowa: Home of the Cass County Historical & Genealogical Society and a bevy of unbelievable amount of Western Iowa history. Some of the most impressive Native American artifacts you'll find anywhere are on display there with jaw-dropping stories. Cass County's is one of the best county museums I've been to in Iowa.

Baxter Cycle in Marne, Iowa: Marne has a population of maybe one hundred souls, but it's home to one of the most internationally renowned motorcycle dealers on planet earth. The most impressive section of the facility is the building that houses Baxter's collection of rare cycles spanning the history of these two-wheeled icons. One stroll through this showroom will make you wonder when Marlon Brando and James Dean will show up and take you for a ride.

OTHER LOCKERS AND MEAT SHOPS IN THE AREA

Minden Meat Market in Minden, Iowa
Rustic Cuts Butcher Shop in Council Bluffs, Iowa

6

LINED UP DOWN THE BLOCK

DAN'S LOCKER

25 NORTHSIDE ROAD, EARLVILLE, IOWA

(DELAWARE COUNTY)

Old US Route 20, or as most folks in Iowa will say, Old 20, spans 333 miles through the state and into Main Streets and business districts in dozens of places, from Dubuque on the Mississippi to Sioux City on the Missouri. One of those small, shining Eastern Iowa towns is Earlville, and its longtime local locker has been bringing business to town since 1947, when it was simply known as the Earlville Locker. It's been Dan's Locker since the 1970s and is keeping up with the custom cuts and waves of sausages.

Johnny Clute was the original owner, and it would become a family enterprise for decades. Eventually, Dan Wheeler took over, and he kept up the quality that this locker was known for. Dan loved the generational regulars that had been showing up in Earlville. Customers remembered Dan as a kid working around the locker; he grew up learning the trade with its old cleavers and knives. He stood by his uncle's side, preparing brats, smoked sausages and fresh sausage and spending countless hours slicing steaks, roasts and chops.

Dan got a kick out of seeing the grandkids of longtime regulars become valued customers themselves. Dan's locker is proof that it's a family tradition for everyone involved, as it is all over the state, from the workers getting the bundles together and the folks ready to load them up at the register.

Pictured here is Dan Wheeler (*center*), the former owner of Dan's in Earlville, with his wonderful crew. He recently sold this longtime Delaware County business and had a great run with selling quality meats in Northeast Iowa. I will always be thankful for the welcoming he and the employees of Dan's gave us.

Opening day for the Former Earlville Locker back in the 1940s. Quite the crowd for a new band of meatcutters in rural Iowa. *Courtesy of Dan's Locker.*

I was welcomed into Dan's like I was one of those generational regulars—another common theme all over Iowa at these institutions. The sounds of the table saw cutting through hard steer bones with ease and other workers trimming ribeye steaks hummed. They all kept working as they looked up and traded smiles with laughter, getting the tasks completed and their cuts of beef packed into the familiar white wrapping. It took only moments to see why the Old 20 travelers and locals have trusted Dan's for decades.

I think about my first time at Dan's every time I know I'm going to be close to Earlville. I also think about the outpouring of fans we encountered on social media when we first highlighted Iowa's Wurst Road Trip. Dan's fans came out of the woodwork from parts of the state that weren't anywhere close to Earlville. The modest facility produces delectable products, and that is what's most important. Let the food do the talking, and all the happy consumers will keep the conversation going wherever they may be.

What we made at home:

Breakfast links sandwiches on toasted rye with over hard eggs, ham, melted cheese and a side of raspberry preserves for dipping
Smoked bratwurst potato casserole with sauerkraut

NEARBY POINTS OF INTEREST

Welcome to Historic U.S. Route 20! EARLVILLE is one of several towns on this timeless highway and is seeing motorists stopping by during the primetime of road tripping season every year. The path from Boston, Massachusetts, to Newport, Oregon, goes through some of Iowa's great small towns like Earlville.

RUTH SUCKOW PARK is a public park in Earlville named after the famous Iowan author. Born in Hawarden, Iowa, back in 1892, Suckow has inspired readers throughout the country, and it is honorable for the City of Earlville to keep her literary history alive by naming a park after her.

The FIELD OF DREAMS in Dyersville, Iowa: This is a no-brainer when visiting Eastern Iowa. It is one of the greatest movie sets in the entire Midwest, and you can play catch, run the bases and start a pick-up game when you're there, just like the actors did during the making of the movie. Perhaps you'll be with the spirits and baseball gods that occupy the lore of this holy land of American diamonds.

NEW VIENNA and LUXEMBOURG: Europe without a passport! Travel through the countryside of Dubuque County and discover some of the most scenic rural driving you'll encounter in the tristate area. The old-world ways and architecture of the area's heritage are on full display with every beautiful mile you travel.

BREITBACH'S COUNTRY DINING in BALLTOWN, Iowa: Iowa's oldest restaurant and one of the best. This is a supper club majesty with some of the greatest Midwest classics on the menu, including irresistible brunches. There's something to be said when you can belly up to a salad bar and load your plate up with cheddar cheese spread, ham salad and local braunschweiger.

OTHER LOCKERS AND MEAT SHOPS IN THE AREA

WHOLESALE MEATS in Dyersville, Iowa
WINTHROP LOCKER in Winthrop, Iowa
EDGEWOOD LOCKER in Edgewood, Iowa

7

EVERYONE HAS HEARD OF THE EDGEWOOD MEAT LOCKER

609 WEST UNION STREET, EDGEWOOD, IOWA

(CLAYTON COUNTY)

Edgewood is quite possibly one of the most well-known lockers in Iowa and Midwest. People all throughout my travels talked of Edgewood Locker as a must-see when they caught wind of Iowa's Wurst Road Trip. When I arrived, the parking lot of this large facility was full, and its popularity was exuding through the buildings. A skull from a steer and one from a deer are displayed over the signage, making the main building feel like you were about to enter a large lodge full of meaty memories. Inside was a busy shopping area and the perfect opportunity to fill up the cooler in the back of my family minivan. Like many of the customers, I grabbed a bushel basket and started picking through Edgewood's large selection of brats and sausages, appreciating the endless plaques that had been awarded to the Edgewood Locker. The years and years of awards are displayed on master-crafted knotty woodwork, keeping up with the lodge feeling one gets from the exterior.

Luke Kerns greeted me, as did Terry Kerns, during one of the short breaks they get on a busy afternoon at the locker. They made time to visit, which is always appreciated because I knew the rush had only begun on a clear Saturday morning. Edgewood Locker was established in 1966 by the same family that operates it to this day. Much has changed for their business

It won't be hard to spot the popular Edgewood Locker when you arrive in Edgewood, Iowa.

in its seven decades of operation, with consistent expansion being the theme for almost sixty years.

The Kerns family purchased a building used by dairy farmers in the 1970s to mark one of their first major expansions, and they kept up the innovation into the '80s and '90s. With growing popularity and the demand for custom meats, the Kernses knew they were going to outgrow the facility they saw blossom through three generations of family ownership. It was time for the Edgewood Locker to take the state-of-the-art leap into the twenty-first century.

In 2019, nearly four thousand deer alone were processed by the Edgewood team. Imagine all of that with other livestock being dropped off from the area's farms plus the meat they use to fill the shelves, coolers and freezers on the salesfloor. Then 2020 hit, and the coronavirus created an even larger demand that Edgewood and everyone with an apron and a trusty filet knife felt. Naturally, they endured the sudden spike in attention and kept up with the demands and altered world we were all living in. They persevered in this small Northeast Iowa town inside one of the most impressive facilities

Edgewood has plenty to choose from on the sales floor. You may want to grab two baskets when you shop here.

you're going to find anywhere—not bad for a place that cut its teeth at a repurposed creamery years ago.

Today you can see the Edgewood team at food festivals and at an array of events that need some well-known and gourmet products to help get attendees through the doors. The team is fun to talk to, but they're also very serious and passionate about what you're taking home. The professional approach that Tom and Joan instituted in 1966 can still be experienced in the 2020s and beyond.

I meant what I said earlier. Anyone who knows meat in Iowa knows about the Edgewood Locker. It keeps expanding and scooping up more delighted customers with every passing season. Since I was there last, Edgewood seems to be expanding its product line to more grocery stores wherever I shop. Juicy brats and footlong hot dogs were getting grilled up by the dozen at the most recent Farmers Day in Jesup, Iowa. All of this is for good reason—they strive to be the best of the best with whatever is thrown at them. This outfit grew out of an old creamery and into hearts, minds and happy stomachs of thousands along the way. There are the popular tourist destinations that stick out with every internet search you pull up when you're researching certain areas for your free time. If Northeast Iowa is on your radar, then make the Edgewood Locker a part of your journey. Not all amusement parks are equipped with roller coasters and games. Some have smokers and legendary sausage, with award-winning jerky being the prize.

What we made at home:

Smoked ham steaks
Blueberry maple brats with homemade blueberry pancakes and a made-from-scratch blueberry syrup
Hot dogs topped with crispy bacon and homemade baked beans
Omelets with smoked sausage filled with cheese and hash browns

NEARBY POINTS OF INTEREST

BACKBONE STATE PARK is just north of the Edgewood Locker, and it's one of Iowa's most popular outdoors destinations. There's no doubt that the Edgewood Locker has seen countless campers and travelers supply up before heading to Backbone.

STRAWBERRY POINT, Iowa: This little town is on your way to Backbone State Park, and it's where you'll find the world's biggest strawberry.

DELAWARE CROSSING SCENIC BYWAY: One of Iowa's many scenic byways cuts through this area of Eastern Iowa. Scenic byways are meant for several stops during a memorable road trip, and you won't be disappointed if you make one at the Edgewood Locker for award-winning meats to bring home or snack on during your drive.

OTHER LOCKERS AND MEAT SHOPS IN THE AREA

ARLINGTON LOCKER in Arlington, Iowa
DAN'S LOCKER in Earlville, Iowa

8

A BRIGHT IDEA AT
THE MINDEN MEAT MARKET

315 MAIN STREET, MINDEN, IOWA

(POTTAWATTAMIE COUNTY)

It was in Protivin, Iowa, where the idea for Iowa's Wurst Road Trip was hatched, and it would be Western Iowa where this book began. Perhaps Jeff Hodges, the owner of the Minden Meat Market, has that effect on travelers. After about twenty minutes of gabbing, I received a tanker full of education during my first visit to this destination that included how many lockers Iowa had during the 1970s and that we were down to just over one hundred in the current era we were living in. When I heard that, I knew my travels to these destinations would be more meaningful from here on out.

Jeff's crew were hunkering down and trimming beef tenderloins and beautifully marbled ribeye steaks when I started to introduce myself. Large plastic bowls of their prized jerky were positioned above one of the meat cases by the register, which created an irresistible impulse buy for anyone ready to make a purchase. Jeff and I talked so much about the history of Iowa's lockers—and his colleagues all over the state—that I realized after I left, we didn't spend nearly as much time on his own business as others. I liked that passion and how someone can go on and on about who he respected and rooted for outside his own four walls. It was in Minden when I truly started to grasp how tight-knit this industry is and how important it is to work together for an even stronger future.

Right: Jeff Hodges standing in front of a large American flag like the Patton of fresh steaks in Minden, Iowa.

Below: That's one way to weigh down the bed of your pickup. A large custom beef order from the great people who helped get it prepared during the several steps they must take before it drives off with the customer.

Minden is a small town not too far from Council Bluffs and Omaha but keeps its rural charm. Before I left, Jeff and his crew had one of the biggest custom beef orders I've seen in my travels. It weighed down an old Ford 150 and was off to a nearby freezer for another customer gearing up for hundreds of memories and good times to come with the meaty haul from Minden.

Pottawattamie County is one of the biggest counties in all of Iowa, with a unique layout when it comes to its communities. The major metro area that is Council Bluffs to the west bordering Omaha is the main draw for visitors to the area. Then there's the rest of the county with sprawling farmland and rural towns peppering the landscape. Minden Meat Market is only one of two lockers in this huge county, which shows you how much of a need there is for more of these local processing facilities in Western Iowa and all over Iowa.

Some of the best moments of locker laughter I've had were heard at Minden Meat Market. Serious stories about the business and its history mixed with a bevy of anecdotes, and playful ribbing paired with the work at hand. To me there is nothing better than seeing that kind of camaraderie mixed with skillful precision on the cutting boards. I'm grateful for every locker and meat shop I've seen, but the Minden Meat Market helped create another spectrum for my constant traveling, and you're experiencing it with every page in this book.

With a sunny Main Street outside calling me back, I made my bratwurst choices and shook hands with Jeff. A big American flag proudly hung from the wall behind him, and one of his workers smiled at his side as he held up one of their shirts. These folks know how to keep the register beeping, with its line of customers eager and ready to get their Minden Meat Market selections back home and onto the kitchen table.

Watching the Pottawattamie County world go by from Main Street in Minden is a therapeutic activity when you want to have relaxing day in Western Iowa. Seeing the elated customers arrive at Jeff's Minden Meat Market is a scene that will never get old. There's opportunity everywhere, and that goes for small communities like this one east of Council Bluffs. The Minden Meat Market crew is showing other entrepreneurs how a business can keep thriving through unprecedented times with strong leadership. Jeff is willing to teach you all you want to know about the meat cutting and sausage business. Just stop in and ask him about it and prepare for an educational moment. Or put on an apron, clock in and get to work, because this place is staying busy like every locker out there.

What we made at home:

Bacon and cheddar bratwurst stroganoff

Ricotta-stuffed pasta with onion and bell pepper brats with a creamy mozzarella sauce

Sliced cotto salami with blue cheese on assorted crackers and sliced Granny Smith apples

NEARBY POINTS OF INTEREST

The COUNCIL BLUFFS and OMAHA metro areas are just down the road from Minden on Interstate 80, loaded with entertainment opportunities and historical stops along the way. Council Bluffs is where the HISTORIC LINCOLN HIGHWAY HERITAGE BYWAY, LOESS HILLS NATIONAL SCENIC BYWAY and the LEWIS & CLARK NATIONAL HISTORIC TRAIL all meet in multiple intersections.

HITCHCOCK NATURE CENTER in HONEY CREEK, Iowa: One of the most beautiful scenic overlooks in Iowa is featured at this nature center nestled inside the Loess Hills within the Old Lincoln Highway path and off the beaten path. It's perfect for hikers, birding, photography and anyone looking for once-in-a-lifetime scenery. This is a view of Iowa you've never imagined.

ARROWHEAD PARK in NEOLA, Iowa: Directly off Interstate 80 but secluded enough to feel like you're in the peace of rural Iowa. Cabins, large cottages, lake, hiking trails, picnic areas, wooded landscapes and plenty of peaceful moments abound at Arrowhead.

OTHER LOCKERS AND MEAT SHOPS IN THE AREA

GRESS LOCKER in Hancock, Iowa

ATLANTIC LOCKER in Atlantic, Iowa

HENNINGSEN'S MEAT PROCESSING in Atlantic, Iowa

EARLING LOCKER in Earling, Iowa

9

THE FIRST OF THE WURST

SKOGLUND MEATS

14 2ND AVENUE NORTHEAST, WEST BEND, IOWA

(KOSSUTH COUNTY)

A late autumn road trip to Northwest Iowa took us to an area of the state that was being explored by our family for the first time. An idea that had been percolating in my head since that summer needed a breakout. We were hugging the Kossuth and Palo Alto County line on our way to West Bend when Iowa's Wurst Road Trip would feature its first locale. It was just down the block from the unbelievable roadside attraction known as the Grotto of the Redemption, the world's largest manmade grotto and the main draw for countless visitors to West Bend, Iowa, year after year. The grotto was the main reason we were there, but there would be another beginning for *The Iowa Gallivant* on that day.

After more than an hour at the grotto, it was time to load up the family and head south. But not until Papa Bear made one more stop in West Bend. The grotto is constructed of rocks, gems, crystals, fossils, shells and stones from every state in the United States and every country in the world and looks somewhat like a coral reef rising from the Northwest Iowa soil. It's a wonder for anyone who loves to marvel at artwork and pure roadside bliss, but we had just enough room for some brats and jerky in the car to start a much-awaited project, and it was time to get moving on it.

Skoglund's would be the first of our wurst and started a common theme I noticed with lockers in Iowa. Many of them are hugging their respective

Above: Visit West Bend, Iowa, for the world's largest grotto and take home some meaty souvenirs from Skoglund Meats.

Left: One of the most historic wieners in Iowa. The Mike's recipe lives on at Skoglund Meats.

county line all over the state. With Palo Alto County just a few steps across the blacktop, we were indeed in Kossuth County, where our wurst adventure ever would finally take flight.

In 1978, Mark and Lori opened the doors to Skoglund Meats, and this West Bend establishment has been welcoming customers for forty-five years. One of the most popular products is Mike's Wieners; folks in the area know them well. The recipe was purchased by the Skoglund crew so the good times can live on with these famous and absolutely delicious wieners. Why did I pick up a package of these? Because the current owner, Ned Skoglund, was telling me all about them, and I wasn't going to just stand there with my mouth watering.

Skoglund Meats is a true Highway 15 oasis of gourmet meat processing with all its selections and other locally made products in the salesroom. Skoglund's ground beef was a part of our meal when we had a family bucket list achievement just a block away from the locker. For years, we wanted to cook a meal at a campsite with the grotto in the backdrop, and we made that happen two summers ago.

It is yet another locker straddling one of Iowa's county lines—one step and you're in Kossuth County and the other step you're in Palo Alto County. I like the idea of eating one of Skoglund's meat sticks while taking a walk in the town of West Bend. It's a peaceful town that I feel drawn to and not just because of the grotto. I've stayed overnight a few times here, and I like that everything is just a short stroll away. Mike's historic wieners sizzling away in a random backyard give the West Bend atmosphere an exceptionally nice touch when you're enjoying an evening constitutional. I'm pretty sure I just described a perfect summer evening in Northwest Iowa.

What we made at home:

Skinless bacon cheddar brats on a soft hoagie roll topped with over easy eggs and pickles
Scrambled egg breakfast skillet with creamy sausage gravy and Doberstein sausage
Mike's Wieners with all the fixings
Campfire ground beef tacos and refried beans at the Grotto of the Redemption

NEARBY POINTS OF INTEREST

The SHRINE OF THE GROTTO OF THE REDEMPTION in West Bend is truly magnificent on every level. It's a wonder of the world, and I can't accurately explain how inspiring this structure is through writing. It's impossible. In my opinion, if there's one Iowa roadside attraction to see it is the grotto in West Bend. I've been there several times and notice something extraordinary every time.

The MALLARD, Iowa mallard: "We're Friendly Ducks" is the motto of Mallard, Iowa, and the welcome sign is roadside attraction gold. A massive mallard is above the welcome sign, and it's impossible to not notice when you're going up or down Highway 4. The town repurposed an old parade float and created one of Iowa's best welcome signs! And mottos if you ask me.

OTHER LOCKERS AND MEAT SHOPS IN THE AREA

CORWITH LOCKER in Corwith, Iowa
RUTHVEN MEAT PROCESSING in Ruthven, Iowa
GREENVILLE LOCKER PLANT in Greenville, Iowa

10

MARK MY WORD

ABOUT MARKS LOCKER

106 ELY STREET, ROWLEY, IOWA

(BUCHANAN COUNTY)

There were two reasons why I originally set sail down the blacktops to Rowley. I was invited to attend the water ball fights during the Rowley Days event and to get a double bacon cheeseburger from the local tavern called Bottoms Up. That's right, reader…I'll travel for just about anything. I mean the burger also had fried jalapeños and special sauce, too. What I wasn't expecting was to be invited into the firehouse for one of the most perfectly smoked center-cut pork tenderloin sandwiches I've ever been handed. The flavors were amazing, and most importantly, it was still incredibly juicy—something you must always be aware of when you're smoking anything for hours.

It made sense that the guy who prepared and smoked the masterpiece between a bun, just before burger time (ouch I was stuffed after that), was a volunteer firefighter and one of the great people who worked at Marks Locker across the street. I vowed that I would return to Rowley and see Marks for myself and get them included within our bratwurst-inspired quest. I managed to get the double bacon cheeseburger down, and thanks for asking.

It was early that winter when we showed back up to Rowley. No sign of volunteer firefighters battling with dueling high-powered hoses over a metallic keg dangling over their heads on a trusty wire. That's summertime behavior in Iowa, and we were wanting ideas on what to start cooking back home.

Three kids and my mother were ushered inside the warm salesroom of Marks and quickly greeted by Tom Taylor and company at the locker. Tom and his wife, Lisa, took over ownership of Marks in 2003 and still keep up with the tradition that's been making legions of customers heading back for more. That tradition dates to the 1950s when Roger and Ruby Marks took over the locker from Roger's parents, Raymond and Velma. Enter Tom Taylor, who started working for the Marks family in the late '70s and became the eventual captain of this Rowley, Iowa staple that lured us back to Buchanan County after one bite of a pork sandwich months earlier. No wonder they've been open for so long!

Tom, like all meat shops and locker owners, didn't shy away from his awards on the wall and was pleased to stand in front of them for a picture. Then the freezers opened, and out came the products they were getting awarded for. A cold Saturday morning was starting to heat up with ideas we were already getting on what to do with everything Tom was unloading into my basket.

I will never grow tired of the stories of people growing up with a family that operates the local locker. Their histories are always unique, but there's a comforting similarity with many of them. The community comes to trust the business and the family that runs the shop, and it's the trust that's handed down just as much as the knowhow of the trade. Marks earned that community confidence decades ago, and the faithful fanbase is grateful.

What we made at home:

Breakfast brats stuffed with potatoes, eggs, bacon and cheese inside a hash brown casserole
Traditional smoked pork chops with fried potatoes and steamed veggies
Smoked pork links with sweet barbecue sauce
Pan-seared traditional brats with sauerkraut, whole-grain spicy mustard, mashed potatoes and gravy, large-curd cottage cheese and cold lager beer

NEARBY POINTS OF INTEREST

Iowa's Largest Frying Pan! Brandon, Iowa, is where you'll find this historic roadside attraction that's just off Interstate 380. It's where you can enjoy the Annual Brandon Cowboy Breakfast in September and get your picture with a giant frying pan in the backdrop.

Independence, Iowa: The county seat of Buchanan County is filled with wonderful Iowa history. The old Wapsipinicon Mill is in the heart of Independence and houses an amazing museum. It's an architectural marvel with a hypnotic view of the Wapsipinicon River rushing by. This city is also home to one of Iowa's best Fourth of July celebrations—it better be with a name like Independence!

OTHER LOCKERS AND MEAT SHOPS IN THE AREA

Janesville Locker in Janesville, Iowa
Fairbank Locker in Fairbank, Iowa
Oran Locker in Oran, Iowa
Winthrop Locker in Winthrop, Iowa
Orly's in Clarksville, Iowa
Gilbertville Locker in Gilbertville, Iowa
Steege's in Cedar Falls, Iowa

11

BRIGHTEN UP YOUR CAMPSITE WITH THE BRIGHTON LOCKER

205 EAST WASHINGTON STREET, BRIGHTON, IOWA

(WASHINGTON COUNTY)

The small business district of Brighton, Iowa, is just a short drive from Lake Darling State Park, and it comes in handy for people needing to supply up when they're camping. That's exactly what we did after meeting Bill Donelson and his staff at the Brighton Meat Locker.

It was hot and getting hotter on a late summer day in Washington County. Cooped up feelings were coursing their way through my head, and it was getting to me. This was 2020 and right in the thick of COVID-19 isolation for many. Our travels were obviously stunted, and it was getting harder to find time to talk with great folks at these places due to the incredible pressure of getting their custom work completed. Many of the local lockers came in clutch when hog livestock had to be culled due to outbreaks of the coronavirus at the large meat processors throughout the Midwest and beyond. To say times were uncertain was an understatement, which means that I'll always value every moment I got to spend with these hardworking folks. Bill brought me in and started showing me around immediately on the sweltering July day.

Bill has been the owner of the Brighton Meat Locker since 2006 and credits his mentor Elle Brooks of nearby Wayland for much of the training he received on the business: "A great, great friend," as Bill described her. He

Quite possibly the most patriotic storefront for a locker in Iowa.

went into his favorite cuts of beef like the Denver steak and his top-selling ribeye steak. His personal favorite is the almighty Tomahawk ribeye, which never looks bad when it hits the grill. Bill also marveled over pork patties and how popular they were with his customers. But he said it was big beef country, and I received an impromptu lesson on how they slaughter and bring the finished product out to the paying public. Tri-tips this, chuck that, front quarter here, under the shoulder and so on. Tradecraft language never sounds dull to me when I start to visit with these professionals.

The German heritage influence on America didn't skip over this area of Washington County, and Bill likes to use old-world flavors in his brats, which is exactly what we took back to our campsite. Brats sizzling under the Iowa summertime sky has a precious feeling no matter where you are or what the social environment is like at the present time. Lake Darling and the Brighton Meat Locker were exactly what we needed—it was already a long year.

A simple Carhartt coat hanging up on a hook near a walk-in freezer seemed to hit a sweet spot for me. I could tell it was a coat that everyone who works at the Brighton Locker puts on before entering the frigid confines of the massive freezer unit. If walls could talk, sure, but what if that

I'm loving the overalls, Bill! This truly did brighten up my day at the Brighton Locker.

hardworking Carhartt could talk? How many hours of labor has that coat put into protecting the Brighton crew from the elements? There's history in every locker when it comes to its four walls, aging and modern equipment showing off their own personalities through heatwaves and power outages. I bet that coat has amazing stories of the Brighton folks lifting thousands of pounds of frozen meats with a few choice words coming out at times. It's a piece of usable and historic artwork if you ask me.

NEARBY POINTS OF INTEREST

As mentioned, LAKE DARLING STATE PARK is just down the road from the Brighton Locker. It's a rural state park that can make you feel miles and miles away from anywhere busy, and you will always find unforgettable sunsets and sunrises while lakeside at this destination.

WASHINGTON, Iowa: The county seat of Washington County showcases a historic town square with all its small-town splendor. Boutiques, restaurants, shops and one of Iowa's most iconic town fountains can be enjoyed in Washington.

CRAWFORDSVILLE, Iowa: OK folks, this one is up for debate, but tell the citizens of this Iowa town it is. They say it's the birthplace of the Republican Party, where delegates met at the Seceder Church in 1854. They were staunch opposers of slavery and created doctrine that later became the basis of the National Republican Party.

RIVERSIDE, Iowa and the future birthplace of James T. Kirk. You read that right. Riverside is making history that hasn't even happened yet. *Star Trek* fans stream into Riverside every year.

OTHER LOCKERS AND MEAT SHOPS IN THE AREA

PACKWOOD LOCKER in Packwood, Iowa
BOYD'S BOLOGNA in Washington, Iowa
BUD'S CUSTOM MEATS in Riverside, Iowa

12

BY GOLLY IT'S GOLLY'S LOCKER

221 SHORT STREET, MAXWELL, IOWA

(STORY COUNTY)

A longtime butcher of Golly's was at the front counter almost as though he was expecting me. I showed up somewhat unannounced after a quick call to make sure they were open on a Saturday morning. I was traveling through Story County and figured I better stop by since I was in the neighborhood.

Tim Hudson said Golly's was established in 1967, with the locker being built out of an old Ford garage. Hudson also said he'd been cutting meat for fifty years and all of it at Golly's in the little town of Maxwell. I was there to hear about some of Golly's best-sellers, and I did. What I wasn't expecting was to hear about their popular smoked cheeses.

I took two large packages of brat patties, which were highly recommended, and a block of smoked American cheese. Plus another block of something that came with a little warning from Tim—I would call it a delightful warning. Spicy smoked pepper jack cheese!

They say you eat with your eyes before your stomach, and sometimes you eat with your schnoz before anything. The cheeses were packing the smoke and had uniformed diamond-shaped marks from the grate they rest on in the smoker—a presentation I will always appreciate. Something tells me the Maxwell locals of old didn't see that coming when they were hustling Ford automobiles in this Central Iowa location.

Tim Hudson lifting two large bags of the Golly's popular brat patties.

An old trophy still making Golly's proud. Tradition of great meats dates back a long time in Maxwell, Iowa.

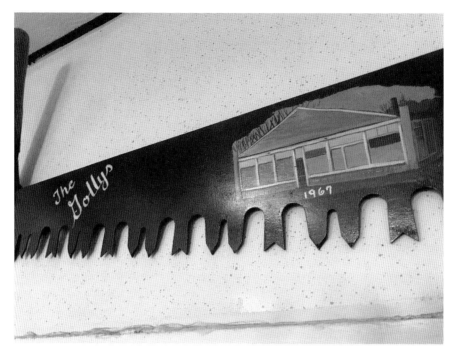

That's a perfect piece of artwork for a locker. A little taste of history on a large saw at Golly's.

I always enjoy listening to the lifers talk about their time at these lockers: the years of changing regulations, ownership and the influence of the ever-changing and fluctuating customer base at each location. Golly's was a breath of fresh air. It is located in one of the smallest communities in the area and stayed busy on the cold Saturday afternoon when I arrived. I came for the brats and added gourmet smoked cheeses to go with them. That's legendary patties going with a recent twist to an old school locker model in Central Iowa.

What we made at home:

Brat patty melts on Texas toast
Spicy smoked mac and cheese

72

NEARBY POINTS OF INTEREST

This is the perfect middle spot between Ames and the Des Moines areas. Take the Huxley and Maxwell exit from Interstate 35 and make your heading for this small town that fills the air with the aroma of its smoked meats and cheeses.

Colo, Iowa, where the Lincoln Highway and the Jefferson Highway meet. It's also known as the Reed-Niland Corner, named after two iconic locals. Colo is a classic road tripper's dream, where two of America's most famous cross-country highways intersect. Needless to say, Colo is an important landmark when it comes to the traveling currents of the United States and especially when our automobile industry was just getting revved up. There was a time when the majority of the country's travelers had a memory of Colo, Iowa, and there are still a motel, diner and museum in an old service station to commemorate these bygone days.

High Trestle Trail: One of the most popular biking trails in Iowa and throughout the Midwest. The modern art masterpiece created around the High Trestle Bridge has brought in thousands of visitors, and it is especially lovely at night when it's illuminated over the historic Des Moines River.

OTHER LOCKERS AND MEAT SHOPS IN THE AREA

State Center Locker in State Center, Iowa
Ridgeport Locker in Boone, Iowa
Mingo Locker in Mingo, Iowa

13

EARLY MORNING

AT THE EARLING LOCKER

102 MAIN STREET, EARLING, IOWA

(SHELBY COUNTY)

Craig Brich and his excited staff were trimming, packing and carrying on with some quick humor when I arrived at the Earling Locker shortly after it opened for the day. Established over fifty years ago with Craig being the third of its owners, this locker is still in its original location on Main Street, Earling. That little factoid harkens back to when communities wanted their locker brethren on the main drag, as they were sure to bring commerce to the crucial business districts of all sizes.

Craig and the employees all agreed that their ground beef was the major attraction to the Earling Locker, so I felt I needed to take some with me. They were proud of the quality, and it tasted great coming off the campfire grill at my campsite on Lake Binder south of Earling later that night.

My cousins and I gathered around the picnic table and smothered our Earling Locker burgers with cheese and all the condiments I could fit in my cooler. Baked beans cooked in the can over the open fire and were scooped up with potato chips from my plate. It was another summer moment of 2020 that was sorely needed. We chose this outdoor spot in the middle of COVID to see each other for the first time all year.

Days before we met at Lake Binder, my hometown of Iowa City, and much of Eastern Iowa, was hit with one of the most destructive storms,

The humble exterior of the Earling Locker with an interior full of quality meats and fun-loving personalities.

It can be rare that you get the entire crew into one picture, but we were able to make it happen in Earling.

called a derecho, the United States has ever seen. After a week of clean-up and finally getting back power, I was able to get back on the county back roads and be with family in Southwest Iowa. We needed a small but much-needed outdoor get-together under the stars of Adams County with Earling Locker's burgers sizzling over a hissing campfire. It was simple, yes, but one of the best meals of that summer: beers, burgers and brats.

Looking at the Western Iowa map, you'll notice how the Earling Locker is on a Shelby County island when it comes to local lockers. In recent years, the locker in nearby Irwin closed, leaving Shelby County with only one remaining in the area and no others very close to this region of West-Central Iowa.

NEARBY POINTS OF INTEREST

While I was here, some of the locals told me about the exorcism of Anna Ecklund in 1912. The whereabouts of the building(s) it happened in are hard to find, and it's not a topic that can be comfortably brought up for obvious reasons. It does bring on curious folks who are fascinated by this story and the book and future blockbuster movie it helped inspire. However, Earling is a beautiful small town with a rich German heritage.

HARLAN, Iowa: Another wonderful town square community with gourmet restaurants and plenty of shopping.

WESTERN SKIES SCENIC BYWAY: One of the best byways in Iowa for featuring the breathtaking farmland scenery in our state.

DENISON, Iowa: Just north of Earling in Crawford County is the birthplace of the legendary actress Donna Reed. Denison is the county seat, where you'll find some delicious authentic taquerias and a lively Uptown district.

OTHER LOCKERS AND MEAT SHOPS IN THE AREA

MINDEN MEAT MARKET in Minden, Iowa

14

ON THE TOWN SQUARE

WITH WEAVER MEATS

204 EAST KANSAS STREET, AFTON, IOWA

(UNION COUNTY)

The town square of Afton, Iowa, was seeing a steady stream of cars and foot traffic when I arrived after getting two large bags of sweet corn from a grower at the local Casey's down the street. It was another summer day of traveling and stopping for essentials in rural Southwest Iowa: brats and roasting ears. I walked through the park in the center of town and into Weaver Meats to shake hands with Kyle Weaver, who owns the busy locker. There were fast-moving employees in the back as I met him.

Kyle went on to tell me how incredibly supportive the community is, and that's why Weaver Meats is a multigenerational family business. Kyle's grandfather started the business as Pettit's Meat Processing in 1975; it eventually became Weaver Meats. The current location was built in front of the original locker and gives the Afton square a wonderful updated look—something that wouldn't have been possible without the supportive community Kyle revered.

In 2013, Kyle took over, and it was 2018 when the shiny new locker we know today was built out. Family members work side by side with Kyle, and they keep the tradition going by making cuts the same way Grandpa did. However, they have some flavors they're working with that weren't commonly utilized when it was Pettit's.

Mr. Weaver himself! He said their bacon was some of the best around, and I wasn't going to turn that down.

Kyle is proud of all their products, but it's the bacon he mentioned first. A package of chipotle lime bacon made it into my cooler, one of Weaver's signature products. Next up was a pack of honey barbecue brats—a flavor profile I hadn't grilled up until I showed up to Afton. I knew we were going to have an interesting and flavorful supper that evening. And it would all be consumed with some of the best sweet corn I took home all summerlong.

Cut just like Grandpa did…That phrase stuck with me. Weaver's has built a modern facility with twenty-first-century knowhow to keep the business model moving forward and added their own twist of flavors to traditional products like bacon and brats. However, Kyle and company keep their own tradition going with the training they received from Grandpa years ago. That care and pride will always be the foundation at this locker on the Afton town square.

What we took home:
Honey barbecue brats cooked on the charcoal grill with caramelized Vidalia onions
Chipotle lime bacon BLTs with avocado

NEARBY POINTS OF INTEREST

This is a book about history, and Union County is absolutely full of it. Nearby CRESTON is the county seat and one of Iowa's most famous railroad towns. It's huge and historic depot is one of the grandest you'll find anywhere in the Midwest. It had a date with the wrecking ball, but the locals were able to save it and restore the old depot that could have been a knockout punch to Creston if the plans proceeded.

Also in Creston are dozens of pieces of public art, including fascinating murals all over town. The city is in the midst of a major renaissance, with many neighborhoods in its uptown district getting an important makeover. Artists of all skill levels are joining the cause to beautify this historic Southwest Iowa hub, including grade school to high school students, up-and-coming artists, local greats and internationally known muralists who can't wait to get to work in Creston.

The MORMON PIONEER TRAIL had its path through Union County and one of its most important settlements along the way. MOUNT PISGAH is a historical site that overlooks a gorgeous valley of farmland as far as the eye can see. There you will learn about this temporary community the migrating Mormons designed to resupply the streams of wagons and carts while growing crops for future endeavors into the West. What was left behind was a cemetery and a monument to all who perished at Mount Pisgah and never made it to the Utah territory. It's one of the most scenic historical landmarks you'll find in the State of Iowa.

Three Mile Lake and Twelve Mile Lake: These rec areas have a unique crown to wear in Iowa. So many people and communities boast about the oldest landmarks in the state within their boundaries, but these two lakes will never be the "oldest." Three Mile and Twelve Mile are the youngest county parks in Iowa, constructed in the 1990s. History is history, and they're bookending our county parks legacy—for now.

OTHER LOCKERS AND MEAT SHOPS IN THE AREA

Corning Meat Processing in Corning, Iowa
Wagner Locker in Winterset, Iowa

LOST WEDDING RING AT JOHNSON LOCKER SERVICE

510 IOWA AVENUE, ESSEX, IOWA

(PAGE COUNTY)

Johnson Locker Service is known for legendary Swedish potato sausage. That right there could get me on the road on its own. The locker was established in the 1940s and has been owned by Beckie Jones since 1990. People drive for miles for their Swedish sausage, and after a statement like that I could see why they were sold out by the time I got there. It would be a short visit because I knew they were slaughtering on that afternoon in the midst of the increased amount of demand at Johnson's and everywhere else in the industry.

The local Swedish heritage is why Johnson's makes endless links of its famous potato sausage made from a recipe that's been passed down for years. George Johnson Sr. opened the business in the same building this locker operates in today. As with every locker, there are tons of stories that can be told, but the first one that came to Beckie's mind was one about a mysterious wedding ring.

It was the 1980s, and a man named Don was working for George Johnson Jr. at the popular Essex, Iowa locker. In Don's haste, he misplaced his wedding ring and was unable to locate it. We can all imagine how hard a conversation he must have had when he returned home that night. The anchor of Don's jewelry collection turned out to be indeed misplaced and

Above: A shelf of keepsakes with the useful gloves you need any time of year when entering the walk-in freezer.

Opposite: Where the flavors of Swedish heritage can be experienced in Essex, Iowa.

not lost—thanks to an amazingly trustworthy customer. Months after Don lost the ring, an envelope showed up at Johnson's; inside was a brief letter and Don's precious wedding ring. It had apparently slipped off his finger and into one of the boxes of meat bundles that the kind customer took home. Don's ring had a little vacation inside a freezer and was safely returned to him by a regular who didn't hesitate to mail it back to Johnson's. That's just one of several reasons why Beckie, and others at Johnson Locker Service, love the small-town feel of Essex.

Needless to say, Beckie and everyone at Johnson Locker Service were running on fumes after a long day of slaughter with more workload than they had been accustomed to. She still had time to make me feel welcomed and had more of those familiar locker laughs that echo all over Iowa.

What we made at home:

Cheeseburgers with ground chuck
Biscuits and gravy with bulk breakfast sausage
Spaghetti sauce with Italian sausage

NEARBY POINTS OF INTEREST

Clarinda, Iowa, is the county seat and home to another phenomenal town square. Some of the best onion rings, at J Bruner's, and pizza, at J's Pizza & Steakhouse, I've had in Southwest Iowa, or anywhere throughout the state, can be enjoyed on that very town square. Along with a fantastic breakfast burrito at Robin's Nest Café. Clarinda is also the birthplace of the legendary Glenn Miller, who was a master conductor in the big band era. His birthplace is right next to the museum that houses so much of his personal history. It also highlights the style of music that took over the United States in the 1930s and into the World War II years, when he was sadly killed at sea while serving in the U.S. Army.

Shenandoah, Iowa, is another music lover's destination we all must visit. It's the childhood home of the Everly Brothers, and their small house is available for you to tour on Shenandoah's main drag. But that's not all you'll see in this thriving business district. The Walk of Fame goes on for blocks, and you'll find yourself looking down most of the time rather than looking up at the classic Shenandoah architecture. The walk of fame features famous Iowans of all sorts ranging from musician, actors, entertainers, writers and politicians to other celebs. Needless to say, I'm keeping my fingers crossed.

Grove Cemetery: South of College Springs near Blanchard is where you'll find this rural cemetery, which gets taken over by the prairie preserve every Spring. This is where you find the grave of Daniel Dow on his family plot. Dow is the only known Revolutionary War veteran buried in the state of Iowa. It was an honor to discover the Dow family plot and watch the sunset come in from the Grove Cemetery.

OTHER LOCKERS AND MEAT SHOPS IN THE AREA

Zeb's in Bedford, Iowa
Corning Meat Processing in Corning, Iowa

16

CAR DEALERSHIP TURNED INTO ZEB'S SMOKEHOUSE

406 MADISON STREET, BEDFORD, IOWA

(TAYLOR COUNTY)

A woman named Brenda and her cousin had just arrived at Zeb's from St. Louis when I showed up to this Bedford, Iowa smokehouse and locker. I was there to talk with the owner, Zeb Schuelke, but I wasn't going to get in the way of customer service, because they made a six-hour drive to pick up their beef order. That's right, folks: Brenda drove their large pickup with two freezers—run by a gas-powered generator in the bed—all the way to Bedford from St. Louis for one major reason. They trust Zeb that much. I knew I was going to be featuring a quality locker just from this short interaction.

I didn't hang around and just watch Zeb, Brenda and her cousin load up the large order of beef bundles into the giant diesel-powered pickup running on idle. I set my notebook down and started loading the freezers, and we all got the job done quickly. Zeb and Brenda thanked me, and back to Missouri the tandem went with hundreds of pounds of beef cuts and an unbelievable amount of one-pound chubs of ground beef. Business was going well at Zeb's Smokehouse.

The word was out on this Southwest Iowa locker, and it was bringing folks from places even farther away than St. Louis. This was also common for the majority of the lockers in Iowa. Zeb and other owners have loyal regulars from thousands of miles away due to their supreme focus on quality. And

A premium smokehouse with Zeb's proud hometown of Beford, Iowa in the reflection.

the outreach was growing from new customers urgently looking for slaughter dates due to their own go-to locker being booked solid for years on out. This is another amazing byproduct of the rediscovery process the nation was going through when it came to the local lockers.

The building Zeb's Smokehouse is located in was originally a car dealership when it was established in 2006, and Zeb said the layout was perfect for the type of business he wanted. You need a large bay door to get shiny automobiles onto the showroom floor, and something like that works well when you're remodeling and need to move in large equipment for a modern locker!

The late Bill Ohrt of Ohrt's Smokehouse in Ionia, Iowa, was the major influence and mentor for Zeb on his path to opening his own smokehouse in Bedford. Zeb's specialties are smoked sausages, skinless brats, deer sticks and much more. He loves serving the community he was born in and, needless to say, was excited to move back. Zeb's even welcomed a camel to be slaughtered at one point and thought it was a joke when the customer first called him. So, you know your place if you're looking for that service!

One of the most impressive and unique attributes at Zeb's is the state-of-the-art mobile slaughter unit it uses. Zeb said his was the first locker in

Zeb is proud of his meats and the merch you can add to your swagger after getting some of those killer deer sticks.

Iowa to have this service. The impressive mobile unit looks like your run-of-the-mill large trailer from the outside, but inside, it looks like nothing I had personally ever seen before. The perks of the Zeb's customer service go a long way—even right up to your own farm.

The scramble was in a full court press during these weeks and months of 2021. People everywhere were willing to go hundreds of miles from their homes to book a slaughter date all over the Midwest. I heard stories of people driving across state lines for reasons like this, but it wasn't until I showed up in Bedford that I saw it in person. I knew how the times were, but it was still somewhat shocking to see it continue as it still is for the majority of the lockers. Zeb was keeping his cool and supplying a clinic on customer service. The St. Louis tandem sped away with hundreds of pound of top-quality beef and the promises they'd be back to Beford again.

What we made at home:

Summer sausage with cheese and crackers
Skinless brats with spicy brown mustard, jalapeños, diced white onion and sauerkraut

NEARBY POINTS OF INTEREST

On the border of ALLENDALE, MISSOURI (Worth County), and ATHELSTAN, IOWA (Taylor County), is one of the most remote historical markers in Iowa. It's on the Sullivan Line, and you must go through Missouri to discover it. It commemorates the HONEY WAR along with the surveying mistake that is the border of the two states. It caused great contention in the 1830s, and war between Missouri and Iowa nearly broke out because of it. Two remote markers on the Taylor-Worth County line will forever keep this historical period relevant, and I encourage all history buffs to locate them.

LAKE OF THREE FIRES STATE PARK: Iowa's state parks will always produce unique scenery and wonderous horizons, with Lake of Three Fires providing these memories in Southwest Iowa. It's a truly secluded state park and offers its own bounty of peacefulness.

OTHER LOCKERS AND MEAT SHOPS IN THE AREA

JOHNSON'S LOCKER in Essex, Iowa

17

LOCKER CELEBRITY AT CORNING MEAT PROCESSING SERVICE

501 DAVIS AVENUE, CORNING, IOWA

(ADAMS COUNTY)

I thought I'd been to a lot of Iowa's lockers, and then I met the man who's been to every single one of them. Dave Walter had his big blue overalls on when I entered Corning Meat Processing at the south end of Corning's vibrant business district and was ready to chat.

Corning Meat Processing was established in 1957 and still operates in its original building. Dave's ownership of the locker spanned over twenty years. He started working hourly in 1985 and eventually became one of the most well-known personalities with fellow locker owners and anyone passionate about cured meats. Dave's father also worked as butcher in the 1960s, so you can say this skill runs in the family bloodline.

There have been times when Dave and company slaughter ostrich among the standard livestock that finds its way into the freezers of the average consumer. Ribeye steaks are one of the biggest sellers, as are the ample variety of brats. Corning's offerings include beef brats, which you don't see in every meat shop and locker.

I had been traveling to Corning since I was an infant and witnessed the community grow its potential to unbelievable opportunities over the past ten plus years. It was the birthplace of Johnny Carson and hometown of my late father and tons of family members. Talking with Dave feels like I've

Dave Walter doing the heavy lifting in Corning. I'll always enjoy chatting it up with this man and soaking in all the knowledge he exudes.

known him for years, and it brings me great comfort to visit Corning Meat Processing whenever I come to town.

The stress of the onslaught of demand matched with labor shortages was showing, yet Dave and Corning's locker continue to endure. The downtown atmosphere is growing, and that's bringing more people into town to shop locally and shake the hand that cuts their steak and packs their brats. Dave Walter is just that man to extend his arm and do just that—along with a huge, genuine smile.

Members of my family were once farmers in Adams County raising cattle and hogs. There's an ingrained appreciation I have for this area and the entire Southwest Iowa region. It's one of the most rural patches of the whole state and never loses its natural beauty along blacktops and dusty gravel roads. So much has changed in the Main Street District of Corning since I was a child. I can't explain how thrilled I am to see the Adams County seat become a model for thriving small towns everywhere while inspiring other economic developers charged with revitalizing their own communities and Main Streets. It's also nice to see the old locker still there among all the recent changes with its long tradition and service to Adams County. I find great comfort in knowing that it's still there and making award-winning products.

NEARBY POINTS OF INTEREST

The Johnny Carson Birthplace Home is in the heart of Corning, a humble home atop a hill with all the historical woodwork and historic design intact within the interior. Sit down on the living room davenport and find the clicker to turn on the tube to watch one of Johnny's classic episodes right there in the home he was born in.

Corning Center for the Fine Arts: One of Iowa's gems when it comes to the long history of local artists, this center has been a haven for folks wanting to perfect their art. Local artists also sell their work in the gallery.

Icarian Villages: South of Corning is where you'll find this French settlement that a utopian society created in Southwest Iowa. The Icarians did their best to keep their traditions alive within a community of farmers. Some of their buildings, like the schoolhouse and meeting hall, are still in use to this day. So is their rhubarb patch, which produces year after year. The Icarian Villages is also one of the best places in all of Southwest Iowa to see a beautiful sunset night after night.

OTHER LOCKERS AND MEAT SHOPS IN THE AREA

Weaver Meats in Afton, Iowa
Johnson's Locker in Essex, Iowa
Atlantic Locker in Atlantic, Iowa
Henningsen's Meat Processing in Atlantic, Iowa

18

MUCH-NEEDED ROAD TRIP TO PACKWOOD LOCKER AND MEATS

117 MAIN STREET, PACKWOOD, IOWA

(JEFFERSON COUNTY)

Another Main Street in Iowa and that's music to my ears. It had been far too long since I just cruised down the blacktops with nothing more than a locker to visit on my plate. It was late July 2020, and endless pasture, soybeans, cornfields and Southeast Iowa horizons were in every direction. My mission was to make a stop in Packwood, Iowa, and drive aimlessly for the rest of the day—my ideal road trip above all others.

Peyton Griener is a young man who raised hogs and would eventually find himself owning Packwood Locker and Meats in 2018. He's the third owner of the locker and doesn't shy away from giving credit where credit is due when it comes to his success. Hog farmer he was and meatcutter he wasn't, and it would be Larry Sample who taught him how to operate a locker. Peyton said, "Larry was the best meatcutter ever, and I couldn't have learned better from anyone else. He had a great style of training, and he's just a great, old-school guy."

Peyton's mentor made quite the impression on him; he learned the craft from one of the area's greats when it came to the locker world. Peyton said that Larry started cutting when he was fifteen years old and worked in this field for fifty years. Sample's education had a noticeable impact on Peyton, and it can be felt every day the Packwood Locker is open for the public.

Main Street in the USA. Packwood, Iowa, has legendary sausages and much more on their piece of Main Street Americana.

Peyton and his employees use all the original recipes that came with the purchase of Packwood Locker and Meats. Their sausages are marveled at by all who shop here, and there was no way Peyton was going to alter the way it is prepared. Smoked ham, deer processing and steaks are some of the other specialties at this locker, with filet mignon being Peyton's favorite cut of steak.

The farmland and its scenery swept me through Jefferson County and Southeast Iowa on that day. A long afternoon of bobbing around blacktops and gravel roads is therapeutic to me with all its countryside splendor. It's nice to be able to enjoy it with tasty jerky from Packwood, Iowa, joining you on the open road.

I got used to meeting with "lifers" or self-proclaimed "old-timers" in this business at many of the lockers I traveled to. I think a lot of them would enjoy talking with the hardworking youngsters like Peyton who are going to be taking this industry into the mid-twentieth century and beyond. Someday Peyton will be the old-timer passing down the skills he received in his early years of owning the Packwood Locker. I predict that he'll still be old school but offer a modernized swager to go with his long story and history ahead.

What we made at home:

Bulk pork sausage made into creamy gravy with mashed potatoes and chicken-fried steak

Ground beef used for hamburger steaks topped with bell peppers, mushrooms and onions

NEARBY POINTS OF INTEREST

FAIRFIELD, Iowa: One of Iowa's best destinations for culinary wonders. A city of around ten thousand, Fairfield is a literal world of flavors with its many restaurants: Indian, American barbecue, Italian, Turkish, Ethiopian, Mexican and much more.

MAHARISHI VEDIC CITY, Iowa: This community is where you'll discover Maharishi International University with its student population that spans the entire globe. The campus was once home to Parsons College, a defunct institution after years of financial scandal that devastated the local Fairfield economy. Years later, the Maharishi way of education and enlightenment brought its teachings to this area of Iowa, forever changing the surrounding community.

OTHER LOCKERS AND MEAT SHOPS IN THE AREA

BOYD'S BOLOGNA in Washington, Iowa
BRIGHTON LOCKER in Brighton, Iowa
BUD'S CUSTOM MEATS in Riverside, Iowa

19

THE WALKER LOCKER LIVES ON

AT NELSON'S MEAT MARKET

1140 OLD MARION ROAD NORTHEAST, CEDAR RAPIDS, IOWA

(LINN COUNTY)

One of the establishments we're featuring that's not in rural Iowa has some roots on the Iowa back roads. Folks in Cedar Rapids have been piling into Nelson's Meat Market since 1935, when it was at its original location on First Avenue. Wier Nelson started the family business, with his son Wier Junior eventually taking over before Jonathan Moore became the current owner of this CR staple.

It is wall-to-wall meat products of all kinds at Nelson's, with sausage being one of the market's main themes. Bratwurst lovers have their heading in Eastern Iowa with many varieties. And I suggest you show up hungry, because Nelson's has a heck of a deli and locals know there's a world of flavors here.

Jonathan's father owned the old Moore's Locker for fifty years in the nearby town of Walker, where so many family memories were made for Jonathan. He learned the skills needed to keep the family passion going into his ownership of Nelson's. Jonathan's uncles and cousins also owned lockers, keeping up with an incredible family tradition.

Before Jonathan took over Nelson's, he was a respected banker and always gave financial advice to other meatcutters and locker owners in the field. Even as a banker, Jonathan made time to butcher for his dad at the Walker locker.

If you want Iowa's butchering history, then you got it at Nelson's.

Old Marion Road with an old friend in Cedar Rapids, Iowa.

Jonathan holding up a picture of his longtime family tradition of butchers.

Nelson's has many historical pictures along the walls, including my personal favorite of this family standing with their prized inventory of fresh poultry. *Courtesy of Nelson's Meat Market.*

Sitting down for a fresh deli sandwich and hot cup of soup has a nostalgic feeling to it at Nelson's Meat Market. The taste of dilled mayo on soft bread with sliced turkey and bacon takes me back to when I was kid living in the Cedar Rapids area. It was a flavor combo that I gravitated to, and you couldn't get dill in your mayo everywhere you went, but you could in CR! It also feels like you're in a time capsule while you enjoy your lunch with pictures of old Big 10 football stadiums on the wall before any of them experienced major expansion.

Jonathan was another enjoyable character I met on the road trip that was inspired by my love of local sausages. The exuberant way he talked about Nelson's and his family's locker in Walker is exactly what any professional traveler is looking for. It's an attitude like this that comes out in the food year after year.

NEARBY POINTS OF INTEREST

The CZECH VILLAGE: This neighborhood has been an important part of the Cedar Rapids history and the American experience of the Czech and Slovak life in this country. This is why the National Czech and Slovak Museum is here and why folks cling to what is left of the traditions passed down through the generations of families that call this metro area home. Unfortunately, the devastating floods of 2008 wiped out much of the historic neighborhoods within the Czech Village, but its central business district remains. Cedar Rapids is a crucial hub for grain processing in the state, with the Czech and Slovak culture very much alive throughout Eastern Iowa.

WALKER, Iowa, is small but still there with proud residents in Linn County. The annual PICKLE DAYS celebration lives on and makes the small town a destination for fairgoers during the Eastern Iowa summers.

OTHER LOCKERS AND MEAT SHOPS IN THE AREA

NEWHALL LOCKER in Newhall, Iowa
RUZICKA'S MEAT PROCESSING in Solon, Iowa
TOMA'S MEAT MARKET in Iowa City, Iowa
LINDLEY LOCKER in Center Junction, Iowa

20

BACK TO OLD HIGHWAY 20 AND THE WINTHROP LOCKER

835 220TH STREET, WINTHROP, IOWA

(BUCHANAN COUNTY)

I gravitate to the old lockers that have stood the test of time more than anything: the ones that made it through the new regulations put forth in the 1970s, the ones that survived the farm crisis of the 1980s and the brave entrepreneurs that said in the middle of closures, "What the hell, let's do it," in the 1990s. It takes guts to open a new business of any type, and that's why I love going to newer lockers with owners that simply follow a passion and the vision that sees a community that will support them in their venture. That teaser leads us to Winthrop, Iowa, home to a modern locker.

The Winthrop Locker's owner had a little smile and a big hand extended when I introduced myself. His name is Nick Wilgenbusch, and I immediately loved his name. It sounded like someone who should operate a meat locker or an offensive lineman who pancakes defenders trying to reach the quarterback. Nick is a self-taught meatcutter and received some of his experience at a local grocery store, which means the Winthrop Locker is a first-generation locker that has a bright future ahead.

Since 2008, the Winthrop Locker has been doing what Iowa lockers do best: taking in local livestock for custom orders, deer processing and creating some of their own classics along the way. I'm talking about the Winthrop Locker bacon, one of those products that's become quite popular with locals and beyond.

Left: Nick Wilgenbusch is setting the foundation for a young locker that's primed to serve the Winthrop community for many years to come.

Below: I was getting close to just saying one of each at the Winthrop Locker. Delicious destination on historic U.S. Route 20.

Nick is another example of youthful presence that's growing in this industry. He and his business partner, Nick Dennie, have also opened a grocery store in Winthrop, which serves another crucial need that small towns all over America are craving. Investing in your hometown, no matter where it is, always creates positive waves, and Winthrop has another terrific family that's producing community leaders. You gotta get the potato salad when you're at Nick's Family Grocery Store. That alone is going to be legendary in Buchanan County.

What we made at home:

Classic breakfast with the Winthrop Locker bacon, including copious amounts of fluffy scrambled eggs, buttery toast, and hash browns
Grilled kielbasa sausage on poppyseed buns served Chicago style

NEARBY POINTS OF INTEREST

CEDAR ROCK STATE PARK: One of the most memorizing and fascinating state parks in all of Iowa. Cedar Rock is where you'll find the WALTER HOUSE, designed by Frank Lloyd Wright. You may never sit inside a home that gives you the vibes that this property exudes. It's positioned along the slow-moving Wapsipinicon River, which exudes the peaceful splendor of Buchanan County. History and architecture aficionados flock to this state park every year, with Frank Lloyd Wright enthusiasts making their pilgrimage to this rural landscape near the small community of QUASQUETON, Iowa. This is where you'll find tranquility at its best in Northeast Iowa.

FONTANA COUNTY PARK near HAZELTON, Iowa: One of the many things that Buchanan County does well is picturesque scenes along its rolling riverbanks. The most iconic of its riverfronts is in Independence—and one of the most well-known in Iowa, I might add—but the bridge and rushing waters at Fontana are just as therapeutic for the soul when observed, if not more.

OTHER LOCKERS AND MEAT SHOPS IN THE AREA

FAIRBANK LOCKER in Fairbank, Iowa
MARKS LOCKER in Rowley, Iowa

21

A PERFECT SCORE FOR

THE IRETON MEAT LOCKER

309 MAIN STREET, IRETON, IOWA

(SIOUX COUNTY)

Abraham was gleeful and beyond grateful that I arrived when I did. He's the owner of the Ireton Locker, and he was dunning a bloody apron and disposable hat over his hairline. Spanish was his first language, but he is fluent in English. The reason he was so excited was because his locker had received yet another perfect score from an inspector who finished his work just moments before I arrived.

Abraham couldn't wait to show me around his proud family business. We walked through every room, and Abraham never once skipped a beat as he talked about everything it specialized in. His family was working through many sides of beef but still exchanged smiles and talked with me as Abrahma and I traded stories on what we knew about meat and the locker business.

Abraham once worked and lived in Storm Lake and could have taken his talents along with his family anywhere. They chose rural Northwest Iowa to build their family business in a town of about six hundred souls. To me, this is the essence of the American dream.

Bloodstained white aprons and pink-tinted white cutting boards were an instant visual I took with me at the Ireton Locker. Next was the gleaming smiles from everyone working there. They all know about the impact they're making on the community with every snap of the wrist. Their families are

Abraham and Margarita at their proud family business, the Ireton Locker. Those smiles didn't leave their faces for a second while I was there.

getting supported, and their goals seem to be getting accomplished. One of my favorite moments to see anywhere is when someone obviously loves their job no matter what their occupation is. These folks love the Ireton Locker, and the very business they keep going is treated like an extension of their beloved family.

NEARBY POINTS OF INTEREST

OAK GROVE STATE PARK: Near the far western Sioux County town of HAWARDEN is this beautiful state park along the banks of the Big Sioux River. There is something fascinating about camping in an area where you can see South Dakota from where you hike or sleep. Western Sioux County has a pioneer feel to it, with Oak Grove serving as wooded area untouched by farming or city sprawl. Sunsets are incredible at this state park.

ORANGE CITY, Iowa: So many people know about the Dutch culture in PELLA, Iowa and its annual TULIP FESTIVAL, and for good reason. But more and more people every year are learning of the long history of the Dutch heritage in Sioux County where Orange City is located. The huge Dutch windmill is the most noticeable site in this historic Northwest Iowa community while the Dutch culture continues from there block by block.

OTHER LOCKERS AND MEAT SHOPS IN THE AREA

WOUDSTRA MEAT MARKET in Orange City, Iowa
BABCOCK LOCKER in Alton, Iowa
GEORGE LOCKER in George, Iowa
REMSEN PROCESSING in Remsen, Iowa
BABCOCK MEAT COMPANY in Sheldon, Iowa

22

WALL OF FAME AT FAIRBANK LOCKER AND PROCESSING

104 GROVE STREET, FAIRBANK, IOWA

(BUCHANAN COUNTY)

Grand champions don't just magically appear when you're gallivanting around. The likelihood of bumping into one in Buchanan County, Iowa, is much more likely when you're on the prowl for some of the best jerky and meat sticks in the Midwest. Just make your heading for Fairbank Locker and Processing in Fairbank, Iowa.

Steve Roffman is a man who doesn't depend on the social media technology that most of us cling to. What he and his crew accomplish day after day goes far enough to keep the steady stream of beloved customers returning and new ones showing up for the first time. Just one sample of the Fairbank meat sticks will get you amped to fill up your basket and whatever size cooler you're traveling with.

Island Park lures your eyes to its direction when you get to Fairbank, and then the large

Old-fashioned signage for a locker keeping up with old fashion tradition while keeping up with its innovations and award winning.

Above: The building that the Fairbank operates in hasn't always been a locker. Here's when it was the Fairbank Creamery. *Courtesy of the Fairbank Locker.*

Left: Steve Roffman with some of the greatest jerky in Iowa. There is no way all of it is making it home when you're driving it around in your car.

nearby white building that's been around since 1903 grabs your attention as well. That white building is the Fairbank Locker, with its interior housing historically amazing meat processing.

What we made at home:

Grilled pineapple brat patties with grilled pineapple rings, sauerkraut, Swiss cheese and spicy jalapeños
Quesadillas with breakfast sausage and cheese curds

NEARBY POINTS OF INTEREST

WAVERLY, Iowa: Another town that's proud to be home to a small college campus bringing students and culture to its community. WARTBURG is a beautiful campus that's a pleasure to walk through even if you're just visiting Waverly.

OELWEIN, Iowa: One of the hubs for Northeast Iowa for travelers and residents alike. It's where you can supply up for your camping trips in nearby FONTANA STATE PARK or start your adventure on scenic blacktops of Fayette County.

OTHER LOCKERS AND MEAT SHOPS IN THE AREA

WINTHROP LOCKER in Winthrop, Iowa
MARKS LOCKER in Rowley, Iowa
ORAN LOCKER in Oran, Iowa
ARLINGTON LOCKER in Arlington, Iowa

23

FAR NORTHWEST IOWA AND

THE GEORGE LOCKER

117 EAST MICHIGAN AVENUE, GEORGE, IOWA

(LYON COUNTY)

By now you've gotten the gist of how 2020 became one of the most unbelievable years and created a food supply monkey wrench for the entire world. Longtime veterans of the industry had never seen anything like it, and there was little anyone could have done about it no matter what their experience was at the time. So how about 2020 being your first year of operation? That's when Bill Punt established the George Locker in George, Iowa, with his sidekick, Luke Harmes, and crew.

Little did this locker know, but it was figuratively answering a bigger bugle call than the founders saw coming. There was already a need for another locker in the area before 2020, and the George community got a huge clutch hitter to help take in some of the onslaught of much-needed slaughtering.

You can't get any farther from Des Moines while still being in Iowa than Lyon County. It's the extreme northwest corner of the state and closer to three other state capitals (Saint Paul, Pierre and Lincoln). Far Northwest Iowa is one of Iowa's beefiest regions when it comes to the amount of cattle being raised in this area. That means there's no shortage of people wanting to book a date to bring in a steer in this corner of Iowa, which includes the Sioux Falls metro area.

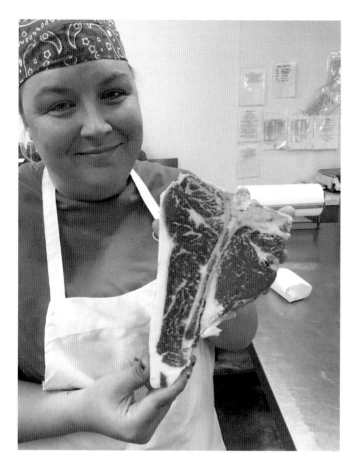

A perfectly marbled and cut T-Bone steak from the George Locker. I hear a grill somewhere that's ready for that delicious beef.

My most recent visit to the George Locker was much like the first one the year prior in 2021. The staff was working with a fever pitch while keeping up with the great sense of humor I knew I'd get treated with again. One person bundled ground beef, and everyone else trimmed sides of beef into multiple cuts of steak and roasts. During my visit, we got on the topic of dried beef and how much I loved another locker's and thought it was some of the best I've ever had. Bill immediately stopped what he was doing, put down his knife, took off his apron, washed his hands and then disappeared into the back. I heard the familiar sound of a latch being opened on a large walk-in cooler, and a few seconds later I heard the heavy door quickly shut and the snap of the same latch. Bill reappeared and handed me a plastic bag that was filled with George's own dried beef. Bill instructed me to try theirs, and I knew where this was going. I pinched off a healthy sample of the beef and smiled. It was excellent—superior to the other place I was talking about. Iowans don't like to brag, but during certain times, it's necessary to pat yourself on the shoulder—or in this case, hand off a one-pound bag of dried beef and get the out-of-towner to change his mind after the previous statement.

George is another small but mighty town in Northwest Iowa when it comes to proud locals. The Lyon County faithful know they're in the far reaches of the state, and they're just fine with that. This county has beautiful parks, lakeside cabins and plenty of campsites for visitors to enjoy the rural atmosphere. I recommend you get to know George and its wonderful locker to get those grills sizzling when you make the dive into far Northwest Iowa.

After visiting the George Locker, we cruised through more of the Lyon County countryside and past the rolling cow pastures and lots that make up the number one industry of the area. Northwest Iowa is without a doubt cow country, and you can see how this local economy can affect the entire state's agricultural economy. It was here in Lyon County where I learned about how rain is as important to cattle's wellbeing as it is to the surrounding crops. It's where I learned how much feed the average steer consumes each day and how much overhead goes into the cost of each and every head they raise. I learned these things lessons by doing one simple thing that many others need to do more often. I stopped at local farms and talked with the producers. Many of them are eager to tell you how the workload operates at their farms, and they appreciate it when folks want to listen.

What we made at home:

Burgers on the campfire
Grilled cheese sandwiches with dried beef on rye

NEARBY POINTS OF INTEREST

GITCHIE MANITOU STATE PRESERVE: Near the town of Larchwood is this preserve with long history and an infamous past. Sometimes recent events overshadow the ancient history of certain areas, and that's what people find out when it comes to Gitchie Manitou State Preserve. It's positioned on the

Big Sioux River along the border of South Dakota just a few miles from the Sioux Falls metro area. It's a landscape that's been home to Native Americans for hundreds of years, with their relics, burial mounds and artifacts still occupying the preserve. Some of the most incredible sunsets in Iowa can be observed here within its hiking trails and horizons. Unfortunately, a brutal act—the murders of local teens—occurred at Gitchie Manitou in 1973, forever linking this preserve to this dark act.

BLOOD RUN NATIONAL HISTORIC LANDMARK: Near Larchwood and just down the road from Gitchie Manitou State Preserve is the splendor of Iowa's plains. Parking my car at Blood Run and hearing the engine go silent is something I can't ever forget. Instantly, you hear the natural wonders of the far Northwest Iowa plains come alive in its ancient majesty. It's one of the few areas that still feels like it was before major western expansion in Iowa, even with Sioux Falls just miles away. The trails are wonderous, as are the grassy hills. The sunny horizons cast a glow all over the valley where the Big Sioux cuts its path southward to the confluence of the great Missouri River in Sioux City, Iowa, hours away. Wildlife is all around you in its sounds and feels during the brief moments you may not visualize it. It's obvious to say that Blood Run National Historic Landmark is one of my favorite landscapes in Iowa. It's more than that. It's one of my most cherished areas I've ever been to anywhere in the United States.

ROCK RAPIDS, Iowa: The county seat of Lyon County, its town motto is "The City of Murals." If you seek public art and magnificent murals, then Rock Rapids needs to be on your list of cities to visit. The history of Rock Rapids is depicted on these murals, and you can follow them through many blocks of the downtown district.

OTHER LOCKERS AND MEAT SHOPS IN THE AREA

FORBES MEAT in Harris, Iowa
JAKE'S MEAT MARKET in Sibley, Iowa

24

TIME TO JET TO JET'S MEAT PROCESSING

10 NINTH STREET NORTHWEST, WAUKON, IOWA

(ALLAMAKEE COUNTY)

Now back to the far Northeast Iowa and Allamakee County! The scenic Driftless area sees a steady stream of tourists, travelers, hunters, fisherman and legions of people who adore the great outdoors. It is truly one of the most stunningly beautiful natural wonders in the Midwest. One of the region's main economic hubs is the city of Waukon, where you find the Thesing family operating Jet's Meat Processing.

Jet's has been showcasing its talents since 1986 with a wide range of products and brat flavors. Andy Thesing's father established this venture, and it's been going strong for almost forty years in its Waukon home. It has won its share of awards for bacon and jerky, among other items. It sells tons of popular ring bologna and those juicy brats I mentioned before.

Jet's also features something that you don't find at every meat shop and locker. Right next door is Jet's Café, where I got one heck of a breakfast. There's nothing better than picking up a list of meats to take home and then exiting stage left to sit down in a small-town café where you can receive a complimentary steam treatment from the heat coming off the biscuits and gravy. My two favorite travel destinations are meat shops and restaurants, which means Jet's holds a giant space in my heart.

What we made at home:

Ring bologna dipped in spicy brown mustard
Smoked sausage links with fried potatoes, red onions and tricolored bell peppers
Bacon-wrapped roasted green chilis stuffed with cream cheese

NEARBY POINTS OF INTEREST

The DRIFTLESS AREA SCENIC BYWAY: This could possibly be the most scenic byway in all of Iowa. The river bluffs will make you wonder if you're still in Iowa with dense tree lines all around you. The Driftless Area is also a sportsman paradise here in the Midwest with anglers, hunters, birding enthusiasts and hikers making the trek here every chance they can get.

YELLOW RIVER STATE FOREST: The Yellow River snakes through the plush forest like a poetic scene you can't possibly imagine until you see it for yourself. Clear trout streams with anglers twisting and turning their lines through the air can be observed while folks on horseback trot by. It has the feeling of being in the middle of a large canyon with the rocky bluffs all around you. But you're indeed still in Iowa, and it will give you an all-new appreciation for the Hawkeye State.

EFFIGY MOUNDS NATIONAL MONUMENT: Near Harpers Ferry, Iowa, is one of the most sacred Native American sites in all of the United States. A beautiful hike will bring you to the summit of the bluffs that will forever protect these ancient mounds along the Upper Mississippi River.

OTHER LOCKERS AND MEAT SHOPS IN THE AREA

CITY MEAT MARKET in New Albin, Iowa

25

DANISH DELIGHTS AT

HENNINGSEN MEAT PROCESSING

1006 WEST SIXTH STREET, ATLANTIC, IOWA

(CASS COUNTY)

The Coca-Cola Capital of Iowa is the City of Atlantic, where you'll find some of the state's best Christmas light displays located on Chestnut Street. Atlantic is also showcasing some Danish heritage at one of the local lockers, where you can get a taste of Denmark without a passport.

Henningsen's was established in 1978 and positioned in the middle of a geographical sweet spot inside Western Iowa: Des Moines to the east and the Omaha/Council Bluffs to the west, with both metro areas being an easy drive away. Now add dozens of rural communities in all directions and you get a handy radius of valued customers that flock to Henningsen's.

In 2017, I walked into Henningsen's for the first time and witnesses a busy locker with a man holding a large electric saw staring down a mammoth side of beef. I asked if I could take a picture of him, and he grinned with his saw at his side. The man was Randy Henningsen, owner of this Atlantic facility with its gourmet Danish selections.

Now, be prepared to read over some of these words a couple times unless you're a Danish aficionado. One of Henningsen's most popular products is the luncheon meat known as *rollepolse*—it gets your Scandinavian palate going even if you're not Scandinavian at all. The other Danish delight I was introduced to was a coiled link of *medisterpolse*. Henningsen's supplies this heritage sausage for the annual Tivoli Fest in Elk Horn, Iowa, where you can behold a huge windmill from Denmark within the Danish Villages. You may not feel like a Viking when you show up to this slice of Western Iowa, but you may feel like one by the time you leave.

My fondest memory of my connection with Henningsen's is when the local newspaper needed a story about the surge of business it was receiving when the pandemic upended everything we knew in our lives. Things were so busy at Henningsen's that the staff didn't have the time to chat for an interview and pointed the reporter in my direction. That's when I knew we were truly making an impact with our travels to lockers throughout the state. The folks at Henningsen's trusted a guy all the way over in Iowa City to explain the challenges they and others were going through. I know they made it through, and when I made my return a year later, I saw that familiar Atlantic sense of humor and blue-collared work ethic on display the entire time I was there. Stepping back into Henningsen's felt like visiting a friend I waited way too long to go see. And like any true friend, we picked up on our conversation right where it left off back in 2019.

What we made at home:

Chorizo sausage and scrambled eggs
Breakfast tacos with crispy bacon
Medisterpolse sausage platter
Brat patties with sweet sauerkraut and horseradish sharp cheddar cheese spread

NEARBY POINTS OF INTEREST

ATLANTIC BOTTLING COMPANY: Like I said, Atlantic is the Coca-Cola Capital of Iowa, and the local bottling company gives tours on occasion. It's a fun yet serious operation, and you must follow the rules given. Have good times and take pictures only when it's permitted. You don't want to be the one that gives away precious trade secrets!

George B. Hitchcock House near Lewis, Iowa: The Underground Railroad had several depots all throughout Iowa, with this stone house, a National Historic Landmark, being one of them. The grounds are beautifully managed and the buildings historically preserved to tell the story of freedom. Freedom seekers from the southern United States were welcomed and hidden from the law and gangs of hunters searching for them before they reached Canada, still a long ways away from rural Western Iowa.

Anita, Iowa: "A Whale of a Town" is the Anita motto, and its welcome signs are some of the most famous in all of Western Iowa. Lake Anita State Park has miles of trails, including a paved path around the lake where you can enjoy more of the Western Iowa scenery that calls to so many.

OTHER LOCKERS AND MEAT SHOPS IN THE AREA

Atlantic Locker in Atlantic, Iowa
Anita Locker in Anita, Iowa
Corning Meat Processing in Corning, Iowa

26

VICTOR'S COMMUNITY LOCKERS

209 WASHINGTON STREET, VICTOR, IOWA

(POWESHIEK COUNTY)

We've featured a swath of shops and lockers that showcase a strong retail business where people can stop in and buy meat even though they haven't brought in any livestock of their own. It's time to meet a place that is custom only, and if you want some steaks, brats or any meaty masterpiece, then you better commit to bringing in the whole darn animal if you want something from Community Lockers in Victor, Iowa.

Roy Stanley has been the owner of Community Lockers for ten years, and the business still resides in its original location in Victor's main business district. Established in 1953, Community Lockers is doing the meat business in an old school way to this day—just a phone number and no website or social media page to be found. Roy gets customers from all over the map, including all the way down in Texas. That tells me that Community Lockers is doing something right when one of its regulars travels from the Lone Star State to get custom orders from the rural Iowa town of Victor.

NEARBY POINTS OF INTEREST

ROLLE BOLLE in downtown Victor: Belgian heritage is alive and well in the small town of Victor thanks to the public Rolle Bolle course and the mural depicting the game that originated in the old country of Belgium.

The "BOHEMIAN ALPS" of VINING, Iowa: The closest thing to the slopes of the Alps in Iowa is in Tama County. Endless hilly roads with winding turns feature scenic pastures throughout the entire drive in this rural Central Iowa landscape.

OTHER LOCKERS AND MEAT SHOPS IN THE AREA

DAYTON'S MEAT PRODUCTS in Malcom, Iowa
NEWHALL LOCKER in Newhall, Iowa

27

FAREWELL WADENA LOCKER

230 SOUTH MILL STREET, WADENA, IOWA

(FAYETTE COUNTY)

I called Tony Harford in 2020 to tell him that I'd like to get the Wadena Locker in a new book I was writing. He was excited and said to bring a twelve-pack of Old Milwaukee when I could make it. August of that year was my scheduled time to stop in, but a derecho storm told me and thousands more to cancel any plans you might have. It wouldn't be until February 2022 that I could commit to a trip up to Fayette County and the Wadena Locker.

I arrived at Wadena and stopped at the local gas station to fill up and fulfil Tony's request. I grabbed a cold twelve-pack of Old Milwaukee and placed it on the counter. The woman working the register said, "If I didn't know better, I'd say you're about to head to the locker." I bellowed with laughter and told her that she was correct. I proceeded to said locker and walked down its stairs. Tony and his friends had already called it a day and had plenty of beers on ice.

The small party was happening on the ground floor of the Wadena Locker. I emptied my cans of Old Milwaukee into a large wooden barrel of ice; Tony was very pleased that I remembered. I cracked one open and tipped my can to everyone there. After some loud jokes and getting to know one another, I went into my typical line of questioning when it came to Tony's locker and its history of award winning. He didn't hold back with what his plans were for his establishment. I happened to arrive on the last fully operational day at the Wadena Locker.

It seemed like a bittersweet moment for Tony. He was boisterous and having a good time, but you could tell that the current environment was weighing on him. The labor issues were eating away at him, and he decided to start reeling it in. The locker business is tough, and it turns into a monstrous endeavor without enough employees.

Tony had been running the Wadena Locker since 2000 and learned a lot from his colleagues at the annual Iowa Meat Processors Association conventions in

Tony with an award winner at the Wadena Locker. Salami with jalapeño and cheese was worth the drive to Fayette County.

Ames. He even took home some awards himself, like one for salami with jalapeños and cheese. I was lucky enough to have some of that salami while we tipped back our cold cans of beer.

The Wadena Locker continued to stay open after I left that day on a limited basis. I was impressed with the optimism Tony still had, and it seemed to be a genuine part of his colorful personality. Having beers with him and his friends after a long day at the locker seemed right, and it brings a soppy grin to my face when I think about it to this day. It's nice to know that there's still a home for Old Milwaukee lovers in Fayette County!

NEARBY POINTS OF INTEREST

RIVER BLUFFS SCENIC BYWAY shows off the beauty of Northeast Iowa with one of the hilliest drives you'll find in the state. The path can fill up an autumn day with intense colors in the tress and wildlife popping out of the woods while you enjoy small town exploring throughout your getaway.

MONTAUK HISTORIC SITE in Clermont, Iowa: You're driving through Fayette County and all of sudden there's an unbelievable mansion with a sprawling green yard around it. This would be the Montauk Historic Site, and it's a must-see when you're road tripping through this scenic area of Northeast Iowa. Go inside and see how it was like to live in this inspiring home, where former Iowa governor William Larrabee resided, back in the 1870s.

OTHER LOCKERS AND MEAT SHOPS IN THE AREA

Arlington Locker in Arlington, Iowa
Oran Locker in Oran, Iowa
Edgewood Locker in Edgewood, Iowa

28

GOODBYE KRAMER SAUSAGE CO.

LA PORTE CITY, IOWA

(BLACK HAWK COUNTY)

Joest and Dan Kramer showed me around Kramer Sausage Co. in the winter of 2018 with energy in their voices and showing excitement for Iowa's Wurst Road Trip. It is, to this day, one of the most enjoyable visits to any meat shop or locker I can remember. I thought I knew about most of the products that Kramer's created, but I was way off, because they showed me a bevy of remarkable meats from this Black Hawk County institution established in June 1964.

That day I took home one of the most impressive arrays of products I've ever bundled up at one of Iowa's meat shops. We made homemade triple-decker chicken salad sandwiches with their flavorful turkey pastrami. The famous smoked turkey legs made a huge appearance on our supper table. We feasted on rich braunschweiger on Triscuit crackers topped with pickled red onions; chipped dried beef and gravy with steamed peas and onions atop toasted marbled rye; bacon, lettuce and tomato wraps with freshly sliced Gala apples inside whole wheat tortillas; mini English muffin pizzas topped with traditional bratwurst, melted cheddar, sliced jalapeños and sauerkraut; smoked pork chops with sautéed mushroom and summer squash topped with sweet red cabbage sauerkraut; and Balkan-style smoked beef sausage with Dijon mustard. Lastly, we snacked on the Kramer's summer sausage with assorted sliced cheeses and Ritz crackers. Did you get all that? It was one of the best visits we've ever had in our travels, and I never imagined the day or the possibility of Kramer's calling it a career.

Heinz and Heidie Kramer opened this La Porte City business with the entire family involved with the operations. This included their three sons: Joest, Dan and Marc. It was all hands on deck because Heinz was still splitting his time between the family sausage company and working at John Deere in nearby Waterloo. Eventually, their sausage company would become successful enough for Heinz to resign from John Deere and continue to build on the momentum they had carved out in the Cedar Valley.

Heinz was born for the sausage and smoked meat industry. He apprenticed in Westrhauderfehn, Northern Germany, at age fourteen. He took his talents to Holland when he was eighteen before immigrating to Canada at age nineteen. Heinz's early twenties finally brought him to Iowa, where his family and business would eventually begin to grow.

Heinz had experience working in the meat industry on two continents and in four different countries, which explains why Kramer's could master so many different products. This included Bosnian-inspired products for the growing immigrant population in the area from the Balkans.

Heinz and Heidie stayed involved with Kramer Sausage Co. well into their eighties. Heinz was hands on with all the equipment and keeping up with repairs and general maintenance. Heidie still worked fifty-plus hours a week and was a constant presence with the customers.

Kramer Sausage Co. was also one of the state's leaders when it came to smoked turkey legs for the Iowa Turkey Federation. The company supplied its popular turkey legs for many events and celebrations, including the Iowa State Fair in Des Moines. Kramer Sausage Co. and its meats seemed to pop up all over Iowa whether you knew it came from its La Porte City home or not. Farmers, hunters, chefs and your everyday consumers grew to love the Kramers.

Kramer Sausage Co had to overcome its biggest hurdle in October 2003 when the original building burned down. Needless to say, it was a devastating event, but the Kramer family made a comeback and got the production up and running once again.

The winter of 2022 marked the end of an era for this La Porte City staple after almost sixty years in operation. That fall, Heinz passed away from natural causes, and the rest of the family decided it was time to move on from Kramer Sausage Co. This news saddened many fans and longtime customers who never imagined a day they couldn't pick up some of Kramer's sausage, brats, jerky, turkey legs, pastrami or a greeting from Heidie.

I feel fortunate to have met the Kramer family and received a sample of what they contributed to the history of Iowa's meats and heritage. They did their part and created some memorable moments at countless supper tables and helped keep the good times going at events all over the Iowa map. Thank you, Kramer family, for getting me to be one of your lifetime fans!

NEARBY POINTS OF INTEREST

La Porte City is within the Cedar Valley metro area, where you can still find a number of lockers and meat shops.

Waterloo, Iowa, has one of the best concentrations of museums in Iowa near its downtown district. The Grout Museum, Sullivan Brothers Iowa Veterans Museum, Waterloo Center for the Arts, John Deere Tractor and Engine Museum and the Dan Gable Wrestling Museum are all within a few miles of one another. This will give you plenty of opportunities to get some museum hopping done the entire day in Waterloo.

The Ice House Museum in Cedar Falls is a fascinating way to see how the area kept up with precious ice demands before electric refrigeration took over. Due to its design, the Ice House maintains a cool temperature all year long, and it especially comes in handy if you're on foot during a summer day. The Ice House Museum hosts a biannual Ice Harvest Festival in the winter months and demonstrates to onlookers how they cut the ice for the area's population. This method is still used to this day, with the local Amish communities assisting with the ice cutting.

OTHER LOCKERS AND MEAT SHOPS IN THE AREA

Gilbertville Locker in Gilbertville, Iowa
Janesville Locker in Janesville, Iowa
Steege's in Cedar Falls, Iowa
Orly's in Clarksville, Iowa

29

SHORT TRIPS WITH TASTY TRADITION

Sometimes we're driving and Iowa's lockers and meat shops seem to pop up out of nowhere. I try to stop at as many as possible, like JAKE'S MEAT MARKET in Sibley, Iowa (Osceola County). Heading to the lakes in Okoboji? You may want to stop at Jake's for those summertime barbecues you're planning.

It was hot—I mean *hot*—when I showed up to Jake's in the middle of a scorching heatwave in Northwest Iowa. Jason Noyes was quickly going from the freezer to customers' vehicles with custom orders of beef with little time to stop for a break. It was just another summertime Saturday morning spent fulfilling orders and making oodles of locals incredibly thankful with their freezers about to be filled up with the custom Jake's meats they have come to love and depend on. However, there was a small break in the action, and Jason took some time to talk and find some historic pictures hanging around the locker. It was another sweaty day in Sibley, but Jason and the crew still made time to talk shop and help a grateful writer traveling through Osceola County. It's moments like this that truly make me so proud and honored to be highlighting the folks in this crucial industry.

Arcadia, Iowa (Carroll County), was our destination for a perfectly cooked ribeye at the SHOP BAR & GRILL, with our steaks getting delivered from Arcadia Meats across the street. That's what I call eating local.

We were on the Western Iowa T-Bone Trail when we showed up to Arcadia, Iowa. This was a promotion I helped to create that showcased

Above: Tucked away in Sibley's main business district, but it's far from hard to find. Especially when you have a steer or hog ready for slaughter.

Left: Loading up another impressive beef order at Jake's in Sibley, Iowa.

all thirty-six counties in the Western Iowa region while highlighting local steakhouses as the headliners. This naturally brought us to local lockers and meat shops all over the Western Iowa map. This brings us to why we showed up to the Shop Bar & Grill. The ribeye steaks we enjoyed there were some of the best we were served on this beef-filled tour of Western Iowa, and knowing they were freshly processed from Arcadia Meats, just outside the restaurant's front door, made them even more desirable.

Carroll, Iowa (Carroll County), is a major hub for travelers cruising down the historic Lincoln Highway. Just off the path within Carroll's main business district is BORDENARO'S MEAT MARKET making its own history. Tom Bordenaro is the owner of the popular shop in the heart of Carroll and his expertise goes back a long way. He worked many years for a major grocery store company and decided to fulfil his dream of owning his own business. A grateful Caroll community is glad he did so because he's slicing up some Western Iowa's best meats.

Bordenaro's was another T-Bone Trail stop that we had to make. Why? Because we needed T-bones for our supper at the campsite we

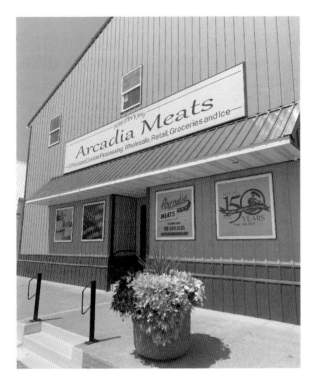

Opposite: The good ol' days of Sibley, Iowa, at the Meat Market. *Courtesy of Jake's Meat Market.*

Left: Arcadia, Iowa's legendary Arcadia Meats!

Below: The family tradition on full display at Arcadia Meats.

were enjoying. And they were huge! The Hausbarn Campground on the outskirts of Manning, Iowa, is where we had a pop-up camper set up for a night in Carroll County. We ate and partied with the Manning locals over multiple grills firing up steaks, pork chops, hot dogs and brats along with an arrangement of stick-to-your-ribs sides. All this was provided by the great workers and meatcutters at Bordenaro's in Carroll, Iowa. The best part about this campsite was having the historic 350-year-old Hausbarn, brought over from Germany, and old Lutheran Church overlooking it.

Opposite: Nice haul, Jay! Beef patty madness at Arcadia Meats.

Above: Bordenaro's bringing an absolute heavyweight to attention with this thick-cut porterhouse steak.

Left: Head to Bloomfield, Iowa (Davis County), for loads of award-winning bacon at Hastings Meat Processing.

Graziano Bros. have been showcasing its famous sausages and smiles like this since 1912 in Des Moines, Iowa.

Hugging the Missouri border is Davis County with a must-have bacon experience. This area of Iowa is known for some of the best deer hunting in the country, which makes HASTINGS MEAT PROCESSING a busy locker for the avid hunters that travel here every year.

My first visit to Davis County was during the Christmas season, and the local communities were alive with festive lights and activities. In the county seat of Bloomfield, Drakesville, Pulaski and the countryside, I bounced from restaurant to restaurant and bar to bar meeting endless locals. I enjoyed breaded pork tenderloins, massive burgers, smoked brisket, large breakfast portions and local handmade candy for two straight days. Why I left I'll never know. Then there was Hastings, where I had the pleasure to take home more of the Southern Iowa food that was so unforgettable.

Sometimes the back roads include the tucked-away neighborhoods of a state's most populated city. And sometimes you may not find any brats. However, I had to include a short visit to one of Iowa's most iconic family businesses and its amazing Italian sausage. We're talking GRAZIANO BROS in Des Moines.

I've traveled the entire country and lived in Iowa, Arizona, Montana, Massachusetts, Florida, South Dakota, Texas and Illinois. Nowhere I've been to and found better Italian sausage than what I grew up having in Iowa. That's Graziano's I'm talking about, and I'm still enjoying it to this day with my own family. It might be a biased outlook on this sausage, since it's been on my dinner table and backyard grill for decades, but I simply haven't had another Italian sausage that compares to it.

Now let's get back to Northwest Iowa for a moment because the air is just right for talking pork belly. Calhoun County is blessed to have three lockers, with one of them being a bacon paradise. We arrived at LOHRVILLE LOCKER SERVICES, and the owners are incredibly proud of all their products, but it was bacon, bacon, bacon when we showed up Lohrville, Iowa. Thick-cut creations of multiple flavors were getting handed to us, and that's never a bad day when that happens. Mark and Carmen have been the owners of this small Northwest Iowa business since 1995, when they opened this haven for folks who need custom meats—especially their famous bacon. Needless to say, we made sure to take some packages of that home. We also tossed in some juicy bacon cheddar brats that we topped with slow-cooked cabbage and—you guessed it—bacon. Next up we made homemade egg rolls with pineapple-stuffed brats and then cheddar brat nachos. The capper was an unforgeable breakfast with scrambled eggs, fried potatoes and Lohrville's ground beef patties with ground bacon mixed inside. The bacon nation just found one of its premier destinations.

30

THE GREAT RETIREMENT

Any era ushering in a sudden amount of change will always be given a nickname, and I heard one that couldn't have been more fitting. During the period of making this book, I heard the phrase "The Great Retirement" in regard to the changing of the meat locker guard in Iowa. At first, I smirked and thought it was clever but didn't really give it much thought. Then I came back to it as time passed by and realized how accurate it was.

Between 2020 and 2023, there have been a slew of retirements all throughout the state, and I began having to go back and forth in my notes to see if there were new owners at some of the places I was highlighting. Sure enough, there were many lockers either switching ownership or closing due to retirement or even health reasons, such as Kramer Sausage Co. in La Porte City. Even in the middle of a booming business, some of the legendary figures were viewing it as a good time to hang up the aprons for good.

I couldn't blame them. The decades leading up to the COVID-19 outbreak were far from easy. I remember thinking when I first started Iowa's Wurst Road Trip, how similar in age many of the locker owners were. The youngsters I've seen at Packwood Locker, Cook's Locker, Winthrop Locker, Frederika Locker, Polachek's and others were somewhat rare. Now don't get me wrong. I'm not saying that most of the locker icons were ready for the rocking chair, but it seemed they were operating within their own generation and bound to start turning off their morning alarm clocks at some point.

It's evident that times are changing, with new, bright-eyed owners taking over some of the longtime institutions that we've been loving for years. I applaud all of you who have made it to the point of your life where you feel comfortable enough to hand the keys over to another person, whether it be someone in your own family, an underling, colleague or otherwise. Many of you have seen the most unpredictable currents imaginable in your tenures, with the majority of you cracking a smile partnered with a grainy laugh.

It's been great reconnecting with some of the lockers that have new ownership—some of which were thrust into "Thunderdome"-like conditions with the onslaught of soaring customers and their needs that come with them. I will miss all the veterans I've met in this industry. I hear some of them are still helping out at the lockers they sold just to lend a hand to keep the momentum steady and profitable. I admire your efforts and the education you passed down to me and others.

It's sad to hear about a locker or meat shop closing, but I'd rather see a longtime owner retire with his or her health than keep it going in hopes that someone may give them a good offer. If you can afford it, the offer to hang it up and start the next chapter of your life is always the best one. I can't wait to hear about some of the shenanigans a few of you are about to get into when you're not staring down a steer or hog every day. But you did a hell of a job when you were!

CLOSING

You know what? "That was the best" is just fine to say. Iowa can have the greatest of something anyone has ever had. Even if others disagree. I've had the best landjager sausage of my life at an old cheese shop in Kalona, Iowa, that closed and has since reopened with new owners. Gone is the landjager sausage though—plenty of squeaky cheese curds left!

The greatest flatiron steak I've ever had was from the Sully Locker in Sully, Iowa. Sure there are steakhouses in other towns and massive cities that would have folks shaking their heads at my claim. But I don't care. Sully's local meatcutters happened to pack up the juiciest and most tender flatiron that's ever hit my cast-iron skillet with sizzling brown butter and fresh thyme. Deal with it and prove me wrong.

The greatest hot dog I've bitten into wasn't in Chicago, New York or Detroit, where some of America's most iconic institutions claim to have the greatest franks and wieners in the world. None of them hold a candle to the hot dogs I took home from the Keota Locker in Keota, Iowa. This Keokuk County staple makes a dog that hits just right, and I'm still wondering where I'll find one better.

I've had countless dishes and desserts that included apples, but the greatest creation I've had with "what keeps the doctor away" comes from the Tipton Locker in Tipton, Iowa. Its apple-filled brats are magical and one of my favorite sides to have with a big breakfast of pancakes, waffles or French toast. Basically, what I'm saying is that when I'm in a syrupy mood I like to add these Tipton brats to the mix.

Sometimes I think about some of the exceptional customer service I've received and that I've observed all over Iowa at its lockers and meat shops—especially at Ruthven Meat Processing in Ruthven. Great attitudes with knowledge exude from the leadership and staff. Every moment in the life of every product could be explained by the workers when I was there, and it made my appreciation soar when it came to this important Ruthven business. A Ruthven business that knows how to support local feeders while getting their influence expanded into nearby Spirit Lake and Arnolds Park. There is nothing better than hearing about an Iowa locker expanding its territory.

The great part of Iowa's local meatcutters is that they're in many small towns and some of our metro area neighborhoods all over the state. There are also opportunities to support these meaty destinations in some of the most popular tourist destinations like Louie's Custom Meats in Clear Lake and Forbes in Okoboji, Amend Packing Company in Des Moines and Golick's Meat Market in Davenport. Whether you're on vacation, enjoying a getaway or passing through, you can experience Iowa's traditions all over the state through these businesses.

You could start throwing darts at an Iowa map, and there's a good chance it sticks on a community that once had a locker or local meat shop. It can be humbling to think of, especially if it's your own hometown that once had its own family-owned business that created its own version of masterful sausages and meat products. There's no telling if Iowa will ever get back to seeing over four hundred lockers processing once again, but there's inspiring progress with the over one hundred we have right now.

Some of the bygone lockers live on a little bit, with their recipes being sold or handed down after they close up shop. Like Mike's Wieners at Skoglund Meats in West Bend. Holly Cross Locker's famous sausage recipe still being used at Wholesale Meats in Dyersville is another example of how family tradition doesn't stop abruptly all the time. It can move to another's and another down the road.

Ray's Locker in Early, Iowa, was started by my grandfather and eventually sold to someone else and then eventually closed its doors for good. Never once did I see it in operation during my lifetime, but the tradition lives on with my family and the memories and skill Grandpa passed down to all of us in his own little way. It could be him showing us how to sharpen a knife. It could be the knowledge of how to cook certain meats perfectly and what cuts he would use and how to prepare them. It could have been business tips whether you asked for one or not. That means Ray's Locker of Sac County,

Iowa, is still going as long as we keep up the practice of all that knowledge and advice that was passed down.

Iowa's Wurst Road Trip created one of the most rewarding endeavors I've ever set sail on during my continual travels. Tender brat patties from the Atlantic Locker that I topped with grilled mushrooms still cross my mind, along with hot links and chili dogs on the Hagge Park campfire from Tiefenthaler's in Holstien; nachos topped with cheddar-stuffed brat from the Lohrville Locker; turkey and sausage dressing sandwiched from Cremer's Grocery in Dubuque; hot dogs that snapped like carrots from the Preston Locker; Blue Moon brats on the grill from Louie's in Clear Lake; smoked ribs on a Saturday morning at Bud's in Riverside where we get our hog head every year to make tamales; brats from the Ventura Locker topped with spicy queso; meeting a master sausage maker at the Newhall Locker; and apple brats from the Tipton locker with homemade waffles. There are so many more culinary creations and endless laughter all over the state, heartbreaking stories paired with blissful endurance, head-scratching business moves with genius innovations and years of family plights along with community triumphs.

I thought of my grandfather throughout while I was writing. I think about how he loved to talk about baseball and how much I cherished his knowledge of its history. I wish I had asked him about the lockers and meat shops of old in Iowa because I know he would have been able to give an impressive list of them. How amazing would it have been to hear his firsthand stories of colleagues raising their own families through the war years after making it through the Great Depression? I can only imagine how hard it would have been on him, and other butchers and locker owners, to hear the news about so many of Iowa's shops closing for good. He was a man who always supported local businesses first and shopped local before it became a catchphrase. He must have seen it coming though and would have helped out as much as possible if he could to spread his influence.

Then I think of how proud he would be to see the uptick in recognition for our talented local butchers and sausage makers. He would get a kick out of anyone stressing the importance of "eat local, drink local, buy local and shop small." I would have given anything to have him by my side as I zigzagged through Iowa while locating the wurst of our state. In a way he was with me all those times because I caught myself saying things that he used to when it came to the topic of fine meats. I catch myself swiping my knife across a steel like he did. I know for a fact that I have an appreciation for the entirety of the livestock that goes to slaughter like he did. I have the same taste in steaks and never shy away when it comes to carving a turkey every Thanksgiving. Grandpa was way better at that, and I don't mind saying it. His locker legacy is still alive even though his shop isn't open and none of his children or grandchildren are working at one. It's still alive because I and other family members cherish and respect these businesses and continue to support them. We carry on, as do countless others everywhere in Iowa and beyond. That's an attitude I'm going to keep and promote for the rest of my days.

I keep giving thanks to so many of you out there who have helped me in this journey of discovery in Iowa. I've loved experiencing the traditions and culture everywhere I go and never grow tired of driving to another location. I get the same kind of excitement with each stop I make, even if I've been to a certain location during multiple visits to town. The flavors of the world are all right here in Iowa, and you don't always have to make reservations at a gourmet restaurant to taste them. They are waiting in sausage form in lockers and historic meat shops everywhere.

I love this industry and always will. I want to hear more of your stories, and I don't want to stop discovering these meaty locales that keep creating their own kind of history. Keep going, cutting, linking, slaughtering, smoking, roasting, casing and slicing, Iowa lockers and markets. You're keeping me and many others on the back roads searching for bratwurst and beyond.

ABOUT THE AUTHOR

Jay "Jay Jay" Goodvin has always told people to never make someone smile when they don't want to. Make 'em laugh! His writing, traveling, history seeking and the constant search for memorable food are what steer his daily life. He is a stunning husband, dad joke aficionado, loyal buddy, shameless storyteller and all-around interesting dude that never got his application completed for *Jeopardy!* He always tells folks that you can't spell routine without *rut* so set your heading in a different direction whenever you can. For many years, you could have caught up with him in some random kitchen in some random locale, and now you must try to catch him during his constant travels in Iowa and beyond. Jay is chief explorer on *The Iowa Gallivant*; host and voice of Iowa Irish in downtown Waterloo; a regular contributor for *Little Village* magazine, *Bread and Butter* magazine and KXEL Radio; and a constant promoter of communities all over the map.

Visit us at
www.historypress.com
....